Windermere and Grasmere

in the Great War

Dedication

For my dad, the late John Tyson Mansergh, schoolteacher; my granddad, Peter William Weightman (1920–2005), scientist; and great-aunts the late Lena Parker (née Tyson), who lived in the cottage Moss Side (now the Lion Cottage) in Grasmere, and the late Sally Sykes (née Tyson) who lived in High Nibthwaite and whose husband Charlie worked for Burlington Slate. Also in memory of their niece Dame Ann Brewer (née Tyson) of Melbourne, who passed away peacefully in 2013.

Your Towns and Cities in the Great War

Windermere and Grasmere
in the Great War

Ruth Mansergh

Pen & Sword
MILITARY

First published in Great Britain in 2017 by
PEN & SWORD MILITARY
An imprint of
Pen & Sword Books Ltd
47 Church Street
Barnsley
South Yorkshire
S70 2AS

ISBN 978-1-47386-402-3

A CIP catalogue record for this book is available from the British Library.

Typeset by Concept, Huddersfield, West Yorkshire HD4 5JL.
Printed and bound in England by CPI Group (UK) Ltd, Croydon CR0 4YY.

Pen & Sword Books Ltd incorporates the imprints of Pen & Sword
Archaeology, Atlas, Aviation, Battleground, Discovery, Family History,
History, Maritime, Military, Naval, Politics, Railways, Select, Social History,
Transport, True Crime, and Claymore Press, Frontline Books, Leo Cooper,
Praetorian Press, Remember When, Seaforth Publishing and Wharncliffe.

For a complete list of Pen & Sword titles please contact
PEN & SWORD BOOKS LIMITED
47 Church Street, Barnsley, South Yorkshire, S70 2AS, England
E-mail: enquiries@pen-and-sword.co.uk
Website: www.pen-and-sword.co.uk

Contents

❦

About the Author &
Acknowledgements

I am a mother of two who has worked as a journalist and as a freelance sub-editor/proofreader. My degree was in English with Social History because of my interest in the history of the north of England. I was educated at Harecroft, Giggleswick and Leeds University.

*   *   *

Thanks to my partner for his computer wizardry with Photoshop. I am also grateful to local historians for their generosity with their research and photos that have been collected over many years, with very special thanks going to author Cyril Pearce, the Lakes Flying Company's director Ian Gee, and to Ian Stuart Nicholson (Whitehaven Archive and Local Studies Centre) for his invaluable help. I have made every effort to contact copyright holders where appropriate and will be happy to update any omissions in any future edition of this book. I have been inspired by a positive attitude towards the Cumbrian towns and villages I have written about for Pen & Sword.

Preface

This book is about Windermere and Grasmere's contribution to the 1914–18 war effort. It is designed to be accessible to all, and for this reason it includes the history of the South Lakes area of Cumbria, where visitors still came for holidays during the Great War. Interesting stories include that of a hydroplane that took off from the waters of Windermere in 1911, rumours that a German airship was operating from a secret base near Grasmere, the double life of Arthur Ransome, and Cumberland Wrestling's post-war boom. Windermere boatmen used their sail-making skills to sew up sandbags, a vital part of the trenches.

The book also has stories of local war dead, including Voluntary Aid Detachment (VAD) nurse Nellie Taylor, railwaymen and gentry, acts as a reference guide to local war memorials (which continue to turn up in the most unlikely places), and a chronological guide to Belgian refugees in South Lakeland. St Martin's next to the Old England Hotel, Windermere has more memorials than any other church in Cumbria, including Carlisle Cathedral.

Introduction

Central Cumbria is a mountain dome, sliced with valleys, rocky or half-barren. Where the valleys open out into the wider lowlands, we find the busy Lakeland tourist towns and villages that include Grasmere, Ambleside, Windermere and Kendal where visitors still came for holidays despite the Great War. 'France and Belgium seemed a long way off, more than "t'oother side o' Kendal", a common measure of distance in the mind of the old folks,' wrote Mary Augusta Ward (née Arnold, 1851–1920), a British novelist, in *Wordsworth's Valley in War-Time* (1915). 'How could one dream of war in this peaceful Grasmere?' she wrote, paying homage to the English countryside and English soldiers.

Since the mid-twentieth century, the village of Windermere (originally called Birthwaite, but the railway company decided to call the station after the lake) has become merged with the older Lakeside town of Bowness-on-Windermere, though the two have quite separate centres. By 1911, the resident population of Bowness and Windermere exceeded 5,000 and this was more than doubled in summer. I will refer to both as Windermere. Windermere (population 8,359 in 2011) and the village of Grasmere (population 1,442 in 2011) are in the South Lakeland district of Cumbria, a county historically split between Cumberland, Westmorland and Lancashire. Historically, Windermere formed part of the border between Lancashire and Westmorland. Ambleside, Grasmere and Kendal were in Westmorland. I have gone to great lengths to cross-check information with dedicated local historians. While historical documents contain valuable information, inaccuracies also appear.

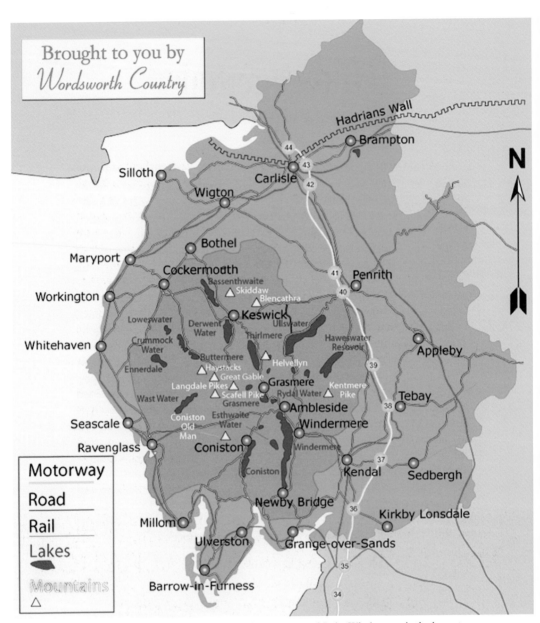

Ambleside lies between Windermere and Grasmere and Lake Windermere is the largest natural lake in England. (*wordsworthcountry.com*)

CHAPTER ONE

Recruits Needed

War was close in July 1914 but Cumberland and Westmorland appeared to continue heedless. However, at 11.00pm on Tuesday, 4 August, Britain declared war on Germany to defend the neutrality of Belgium. Four days later, Westmorland Territorial Army soldiers paraded, excitedly, towards Kendal railway station where virtually all the local gentry, the corporation and magistrates were assembled. Tom Gordon Thompson, elected mayor of Kendal for a second time in 1914, assured the men that their dependants would be well looked after. Public notices and comments on wartime restrictions and events featured strongly in the *Westmorland Gazette* (hereafter *WG*) of 8 August, though advertisements were still being published for recreational journeys. The following week, an advertisement in the *WG* by a Kendal wool shop offered 'Khaki Wool for knitting helmets, scarves, bed socks and other useful articles for our brave soldiers'.

Many reckoned that the war would be over by Christmas, the 'Hun' being rapidly beaten by the gallant British troops with minimal losses. German commanders tended to think that Britain's entry into the war would make little difference. Britannia certainly ruled the waves with the world's largest navy but as the Kaiser put it, 'dreadnoughts have no

The European Conflagration: How the *Westmorland Gazette* reported the declaration of war in August 1914. (Westmorland Gazette)

THE WESTMORLAND G.

THE EUROPEAN CONFLAGRATION.

GERMAN INVASION OF BELGIUM.

A BRITISH ULTIMATUM : WAR DECLARED.

Fighting Begun : Germans Repulsed near Liege.

British Navy Active in the North Sea.

Germany declared war on England at seven numerous proofs of your Majesty's friendship, mines can be fastened round the bulwarks or, wheels'. Unlike Britain, all the continental powers had huge armies, enrolled or formed by conscription. (Conscription had been an accepted part of German society for decades prior to 1914.) In 1914, the British army consisted of just over 730,000 officers and men. One-third served in the regular army, with the greater part stationed in reserve formations, the most notable of which was the Territorial Force (TF), subsequently becoming the Territorial Army (TA).

King's Own

On the outbreak of war, the King's Own (KO) Royal Lancaster Regiment was made up of two Regular battalions (the 1st and 2nd Battalion) and two Territorial battalions, as well as a Special Reserve Battalion. By the end of the war, the KO had expanded to seventeen battalions. During the war, more than 44,000 men served with the KO Regiment, of whom 7,000 died.

On Sunday, 2 August 1914, the 4th Battalion proceeded to camp at Kirkby Lonsdale, near Kendal, to undergo the usual fourteen days' annual training as one of the units forming the West Lancashire Brigade of the Territorial Force. War and rumours of war then filled the air. Upon arrival at Kirkby Lonsdale, a warning was issued by Colonel Godfrey Leicester Hibbert DSO (Distinguished Service Order), Commanding North Lancashire Infantry Brigade, for the units comprising the brigade not to make themselves too comfortable nor to make preparations for any lengthy stay. The warning was issued as orders had been received to detain the trains in which the troops had arrived, and further orders for the troops to return to their peace stations were expected. These orders duly arrived in the early hours of Monday, 3 August. At 9.30am, the battalion started on its homeward journey after the shortest annual training period on record.

The 4th Battalion of the pre-war TF became the 1/4th Battalion TF. The 1/4th Battalion TF was mobilized at the important shipbuilding town of Barrow-in-Furness, about 25 miles from Windermere, on 4 August 1914. The following day, it left to guard the Kent and Leven Viaducts, the Duddon Viaduct and to protect the works of Vickers shipyard, Barrow and the harbour and docks of the Furness Railway Company, Barrow. The surplus men not required for guards were billeted in the Holker Street Schools, Barrow.

The battalion left for Ulverston billets (the Barrow defences were taken over by another battalion) on 11 August and for Slough, Berkshire on 15 August to guard the stations on the length of railway line from Paddington to Twyford, and then trained in Kent and Bedford. On the afternoon of 3 May 1915, the battalion – though not as a complete unit

Officers of the 1/4th Battalion at Bedford before proceeding overseas on 3 May 1915.
Back row, L to R: 2nd Lts James Fisher, Harry Robert Sykes, Harold Arthur
Brocklebank, R.H. Steinthal, Edward Spearing; Lts Geoffrey Fell Taylor, E.H. Hewitt,
who was killed at Festubert on 16 June 1915; Capt. Alexander Allen Wright, killed on
the Somme on 8 August 1916; 2nd Lt William Campbell Neill, Lt John Fisher, who
became staff captain in December 1915; and 2nd Lt Thomas William Dugdale.
Middle row, L to R: Lt Col. Robert Gardner, who arrived in Ulverston on 11 June 1919
met by an enthusiastic crowd; Lt James Crossley (Quartermaster), who returned to
England for a rest on 7 May 1917 after two years at the front; Capts W. Garencieres
Pearson, James Vince Barrow, George B. Balfour, J.M. Mawson, Ralph D'Albini
Morrell, who lived in The Beeches, Grange and was killed on the Somme on 8 August
1916; Lt H.Y. Huthwaite, who reported sick at Ypres on 30 November 1916 and was
transferred to England and later to the Indian army; Lt George Henry Walker; and
2nd Lt George Braddyll Bigland.
Front row, L to R: Capt. W.D. Barrett; Medical Officer Maj. A.F. Rutherford;
Maj. R. Thompson (second-in-command); Lt Col. W.F.A. Wadham (Commanding),
who eventually returned to England on medical grounds and wrote *The Fourth Battalion
The King's Own and The Great War* (1920); Captain V.A. Jackson (Adjutant);
Maj. Nicholas E. Barnes, who was in command of the battalion on 20 January 1916
when the CO went on short leave and arrived in Ulverston on 11 June 1919 met by an
enthusiastic crowd; and Capt. R.P. Little. (*The King's Own Royal Regiment Museum, Lancaster*)

as it had been called on to provide guards in the UK – left Bedford for
the Western Front via Folkestone and Boulogne. The night of 24/25 May
1915 marked its first introduction to the trenches in the neighbourhood
of Richebourg-l'Avoué, France. During the Battle of Festubert in
France on 15 June 1915, the battalion emerged depleted in strength.

Border Regiment

The Border Regiment (1881–1959), based in Carlisle and named after England's border with Scotland, was only five battalions in strength – two regular, one reserve (3rd) and two Territorial Force – on the outbreak of the Great War. The 2nd Battalion (regular) was mobilized for war on 6 October 1914. In its first encounter with the enemy at Kruiseik Hill, Belgium – captured by the Germans on 29 October 1914 and in their hands until 28 September 1918 – the men of the 2nd Battalion were surrounded in their trenches on three sides by the enemy.

As the conflict progressed, the Border Regiment expanded to form sixteen battalions. Seven of the regiment's battalions took part in the Battle of the Somme (1 July to 18 November 1916 on both sides of the River Somme), in which the British army suffered 420,000 casualties; the long Battle of the Somme showed that there would be no early or easy victory. According to the *Cumberland News* of 18 November 1922, the Border Regiment Roll of Honour (ROH) at Carlisle Cathedral lists 6,200 dead of the Great War.

Joining up with friends

With conscription politically unpalatable, Lord Kitchener (1850–1916), the newly-appointed Secretary of State for War, decided to raise a New Army of volunteers. Men were invited to volunteer with their friends, family and colleagues to form the Pals battalions. The idea was that men were more likely to join up to fight if they did so alongside people they knew, especially in the industrial north. With the introduction of conscription in January 1916, further Pals battalions were not sought.

The 8th (Service) Battalion, Border Regiment (Kendal Pals) was formed in August 1914, and men were recruited in Keswick, Kendal and Windermere. There is a photograph in the *WG* in May 1915 of 'all fifteen men with 8th Border'. Lists printed in June 1915 indicate numbers in the region of six from Grasmere and sixteen from Ambleside had enlisted. A total of thirteen men from Windermere, Grasmere and Ambleside died while serving with the 8th Border.

The 8th Battalion was moved to Codford Camp, Salisbury Plain for training in November 1914, billeted in Boscombe. It was moved to Romsey in May 1915 and on to Aldershot the following month. It arrived at Boulogne on 27 September 1915, was moved to billets at Le Bizet by 29 September and soon began visiting the front line trenches, a couple of miles east of Ploegsteert, Belgium. This area was a 'quiet' portion of the Western Front, much used by the British army as a training area for newly-arrived units, but it was still a very dangerous place with frequent very heavy enemy artillery bombardments and more than usually

Kendal Pals in early training at Kendal Castle.
(Courtesy of Paul Bramham, freewebs.com/kendal pals)

Members of the Kendal Pals in a captured German trench during the Somme offensive.
The photo, taken at Ovillers on 15 July 1916, was a postcard from a series taken by
Daily Mail photographers. (Westmorland Gazette)

Pozières British Cemetery, Ovillers-la-Boisselle. Eight members of the Border Regiment are buried here, seven of them Kendal Pals: Private F.J. Barnes, Private W. Cockton, Private Wilfred Lawson Coombes, Private J. Cunliffe, Corporal E. Hold, Private Sidney Herbert Pearson and Lance Corporal J.B. Rose. *(cwgc.org)*

A group of Kendal Pals at Bournemouth. Standing: J. Ruthven, B. Jeffreys, J.H. Ruthven, W.D. Waller, E. Jeffreys. Sitting: E. Heatherington, E. Tattersall, J. Birtwhistle, Alfred R. Sill, J. Procter [more likely Proctor but reproduced as in the original newspaper caption]. *(Westmorland Gazette)*

active German snipers. The 8th Battalion remained in the area around Ploegsteert for four months. During this period, fourteen of their officers and men were killed or died of their wounds. More than 300 Kendal Pals were killed on the Somme. More of them are buried in Warloy-Baillon or Puchevillers than Pozières.

Lonsdale Pals

Lord Lonsdale Hugh Cecil Lowther – whose wealth was derived from the West Cumberland coal mines – had a residence at Lowther Castle, Penrith and a hunting lodge overlooking Lake Windermere, Holbeck Ghyll. Both the Kaiser and King George V stayed at Holbeck Ghyll while out hunting with him. Later, he would go on to form his own battalion, named after him, to fight the Kaiser. When he motored to the Brough Hill Fair, a gypsy gathering in Westmorland, on 1 October 1917, he was asked by a local preacher what he thought of his friend the Kaiser now. The reply was not caught, but it was not lacking in vigour (*Yorkshire Evening Post*, 2 October 1917). In April 1918, he said he 'would love the chance to catch the emperor'.

The 11th (Service) Battalion Border Regiment (Lonsdales) – local men drawn from the railways, factories, shops and fields of Cumberland and Westmorland – was formed in Penrith (HQ), Carlisle, Kendal and Workington on 17 September 1914, and Windermere and Grasmere men served with the Lonsdales. Seven were born in Windermere, seven were born in Keswick and fourteen enlisted in Windermere.

The Lonsdale ROH exists online (border-regiment-forum.com), in book form and as a CD *Soldiers Died in the Great War*. It was transcribed exactly as it was printed in HMSO's *Soldiers Died in the Great War, Volume 39, The Border Regiment*. The Lonsdale ROH lists only those who died.

Holbeck Ghyll, bought by Lord Lonsdale in 1888, has been a hotel since the 1970s. (*holbeckghyll.com*)

Lord Lonsdale took a great deal of pride in the battalion, paid for their equipment with his own money, and issued the men with a solid silver hallmarked cap badge that he commissioned. He planned 'his' uniform to be of hodden grey, perhaps forgetting that the Germans had already taken up that option (in 1910). On 11 September 1914, D. Morphy & Co. of Kendal had secured sufficient army grey flannel for Lord Lonsdale to make 1,000 men's shirts and could make and deliver these the following week. However, the War Office said Lord Lonsdale's uniform had to be khaki. Cumbria Archives has a reference to R.W. & T.K. Thompson, merchant tailors of Carlisle, supplying shirts. There is a note about quantity 'to be made in Kendal'. Other documents name Wilson Jespers & Co. of English Street, Carlisle as supplying khaki shirts. One letter at Cumbria Archives talks of instructing Waddells (Cumberland Mill, Warwick Bridge) to cease production of grey and commence production of khaki.

On 5 January 1915, the Kendal detachment of the Lonsdale Battalion in their grey uniforms left Kendal for their new quarters at Carlisle. The station platform was crowded with relatives and other well-wishers to see them off. They trained on Blackwell Racecourse on the edge of Carlisle. Initially, conditions at Blackwell Racecourse were so inadequate that soldiers who could return would go back home to sleep at night. Those who could not made themselves as comfortable as they could in the empty horse boxes and grandstand. Eventually, wooden huts were erected. In November 1914, St George's Theatre, Kendal showed all week a special local picture secured at Blackwell Racecourse, *A Day with the Lonsdale Battalion*. Scenes included physical and company drill, full parade, dinner time and preparing meals. However, this must have been a little frustrating for the men of the Kendal detachment whose departure had been delayed for logistical reasons and they were therefore absent from the film. The Lonsdales did a lot of trench-digging there. On 3 January 1915, the Lonsdale Battalion had attained a total strength of 1,152 non-commissioned officers and men. By March 1915, it had swelled to 1,350 – the full strength authorized – and on 8 May, a tremendous crowd at Carlisle railway station saw the men off and the battalion moved to Prees Heath Camp, Shropshire, dress khaki. Battalion orders on 16 March 1915 stated: 'Officers Commanding Companies must be very particular to see that no alterations are made in the new Khaki Clothing. There is always a tendency for young soldiers to desire to have their clothing made so tight as to make it impossible for them to move their limbs freely.'

The battalion would ultimately set sail for France on 23 November 1915. On the opening day of the Battle of the Somme, 1 July 1916, the

Make do and mend: soldiers training on Blackwell Racecourse, Carlisle in March 1916.
The soldiers lacked even basic equipment such as a rifle and a uniform until 1915.
(*Public domain*)

Lonsdales suffered more than 500 casualties out of the 800 who went
into action, according to Cumbria's Museum of Military Life. The Lonsdales spent two years and eight months on the Western Front. Lord
Lonsdale said at a presentation in Penrith reported in the *Penrith
Observer* on 16 April 1918: 'The object – it sounded a brutal one, but it
was the only way we could compete with the enemy – was the destruction of the enemy.' He also deeply regretted that any friend he ever had
should be responsible for such frightful atrocities as had been
committed.

Sergeant Joshua Hardisty (1882–1916), 11th Border, enlisted in
Ambleside and was the first Grasmere man to join the Lonsdales; he was
killed in action (Western Front) on 18 November 1916. A painter in
Grasmere, he was one of four sons of Henry (1845–1922) and Mary Ann
Hardisty (née Norman, 1855–1926) of Turn Howe, Grasmere in active
service. He was awarded the Military Medal for gallantry, his body lies
in Waggon Road Cemetery and he is remembered on the slate tablet
inside St Oswald's Church, Grasmere. His brother Private John Hardisty
(1885–1916), 1st Border, was killed in action, probably near Ypres,
on 30 July 1916 and is also remembered on the slate tablet inside
St Oswald's. He married Mary Nelson in 1911 and they had two children
during their marriage.

At the time of the men's death, Reverend Hardwick Drummond
Rawnsley (1881–1920), who was moved to St Kentigern's Church, Crosthwaite, Keswick in 1883, was living at Allen Bank, Grasmere. Following the death of Joshua, he wrote a poem for their grieving mother:

To the mother of 4 sons gone to the war, 1914–1918
by Canon Rawnsley

Sgt, Hardisty M.M, 11th Battalion Border Regiment.
Fell in action Nov. 18th
John Hardisty 1st Border Regiment.
Fell in action July 10th 1916
Two brothers Harry & Walter still at the front.

Mother of 4 sons gone to war,
Hark how the stream mourns loud in the hollow.
Two have fallen in fields afar
Two still the foremen follow.

Was it for this you reared each boy,
In the calm of the dale and peace of the Mountains,
For this their young hearts leapt with joy,
And rush of Greenburns fountains.

For this that the borrowed strength of the hills.
And the freedom born of the torrents foaming,
That sycamore buds and the daffodils,
And cuckoo's call at gloaming.

So nursed in their hearts the love of home
That swift when they heard England's calling
They answered 'O Mother, we come, we come.'
Left painters work and walling.

For this in defence of Grasmere Vale
They topped the parapet, bombed trenches
Endured the terrible shrapnel hail
Blood, mud and battle stenches.

For this, from the cottage beneath Helm Crag
And not for the sake of a medal's glory
They went to offer their lives for the flag
And honour's ancient story.

Weep not Mother, rejoice with pride
No more the stream mourns loud in the hollow
But it roars applause for the twain who died
And the twain who the lads follow.

W.H. Rawnsley
Allan Bank
Grasmere.

Note Mrs Hardisty's youngest son is now in training.

A bunch of Grasmere lads. Back row, L to R: Peter Sanderson, Henry Hardisty, Jacko Wilson, Sydney Fletcher, Walter Hardisty. Front row, L to R: Jimmy Sanderson, Henry Smith, Ernie C., Alf Nicholson, Alfred Marsden. (*cumbrianwarmemorials*)

Walter Hardisty, born in 1894 in Langdale, a valley that was one of the centres of the Lakeland slate industry, married in 1932 and died in Grasmere in 1981. Henry and Mary Ann's other sons were Charles Norman Hardisty (1884–1960), born in Seascale in west Cumbria; Henry Hardisty (b.1890), born in Seascale; and James Coalbank Hardisty (1899–1994), born in Grasmere. Charles emigrated to the US from Grasmere in 1907 (on RMS *Umbria*). Henry and Mary Ann had two daughters, Sarah Ada (1887–1978), born in Seascale, and Mary Dinah (b.1892), born in Langdale. Mary emigrated to the US from Grasmere in 1912 (on RMS *Mauretania*). Sarah married George Stamper and they had a son, Thomas.

CHAPTER TWO

The Battle for the Skies

Windermere's cultural history and heritage is not all about tourism, nor the industrialists from Manchester who chose to build grand summer mansions dug into the wood-slopes around Lake Windermere as poor country people migrated to the 'dark satanic mills' of the Industrial Revolution seeking employment.

Barrister landowner Captain Edward Wakefield (1862–1941) of Kendal and Oscar Gnosspelius (1878–1953), whose home was Silverholme Manor (now a hotel) on the western shore of Lake Windermere, were independently inspired to investigate the possibilities of flying from water after visiting the 1909 Aviation Meeting in Blackpool (seven days of changeable weather in October) about pioneering a new sport of flying (see *Flight* magazine, October 1909).

The world's first successful flights from water were made by Henri Fabre (1882–1984) of France on 28 March 1910 and by the American founder of the US aircraft industry Glenn Curtiss (1878–1930) on 26 January 1911. Edward Wakefield ordered an aeroplane of similar design to Curtiss's from A.V. Roe & Co. (*aka* Avro) of Brownsfield Mills, Manchester. The hydroplane, subsequently named Waterbird, was brought to Windermere in July 1911 to be fitted with floats made by Borwick & Sons (since taken over by Windermere Aquatic).

In the early morning of 25 November 1911, Edward Wakefield's pilot Herbert Stanley Adams (1880–1948) took Waterbird out on to the lake from Hill of Oaks (land belonging to Wakefield) and successfully flew at a height of 50ft from Hill of Oaks to Ferry Nab and back, alighting safely. Edward Wakefield, with Adams as his pilot, had achieved the first successful flight from water in the British Empire.

Gnosspelius (who during the First World War was commissioned in the Royal Naval Air Service (RNAS), later Royal Air Force (RAF), and was employed on the inspection staff) carried out his experiments at Bowness Bay with his friend and boat-builder Arthur Borwick. He flew his hydroplane Gnosspelius No. 2 from Windermere on the same morning as Waterbird's first flight. However, he could not maintain control and crashed on landing when Gnosspelius No. 2 flipped onto its back

(*Left*) The original Waterbird taking off from Windermere. (Westmorland Gazette)
(*Right*) Pilot Herbert Stanley Adams. (*Courtesy of Frank Herbert*)

(but he later succeeded on 14 February 1912). Gnosspelius, a friend of the author Arthur Ransome, was able to climb out unhurt and was rescued. He died in February 1953 and is buried in Coniston Cemetery.

Waterbird flew intensively during December 1911 and January 1912, logging sixty flights; the longest was for 20 miles, reaching a height of 800ft. Unfortunately, in March 1912 Waterbird was destroyed in its lakeside hangar by a storm. It was succeeded by the Lakes-built Waterhen, a design drawn up for Wakefield by Gnosspelius, incorporating the lessons learned with Waterbird. Passenger flights were later available in Waterhen at a price of 2 guineas.

On 16 April 1912, Winston Churchill, then First Lord of the Admiralty, confirmed in the House of Commons that hydroplane tests would continue on Windermere. His confirmation was in response to a question raised by Russell Rea (1846–1916), who was against flying at Windermere. Rea, whose father Daniel Key Rea was from Eskdale, was a privately-educated English ship-owner from Liverpool and a Liberal Party politician.

Aeroplanes that flew at Windermere between 1911 and 1919 included Waterbird, Gnosspelius No. 2, Waterhen, Deperdussin, Avro Duigan (D)/Seabird, Avro 501, Gnosspelius-Trotter, Lakes Monoplane, Blériot, Blackburn Improved Type 1, PB 1, Nieuport, FBAs, Sopwith Schneider, Shorts 827s and Avro 504s (the Lakes Flying Company). On 2 April 1912, British pioneer aviator Sydney Vincent Sippe (1889–1968) flew the Avro D from Barrow dock successfully, the first flight from seawater in Britain. He flew an Avro 504 on 21 November 1914 during an RNAS raid on the Zeppelin sheds and factories near Friedrichshafen in

Edward Wakefield at the joystick in his precarious 'cockpit'. (*Courtesy of Frank Herbert*)

Sippe learned to fly at the Avro School at Brooklands, Surrey.
(*Courtesy of the Lakes Flying Company*)

southern Germany, the Friedrichshafen Raid. One pilot was shot down and captured but Sippe and the third pilot returned safely.

Aeronautical pioneer Gertrude Bacon (1874–1949), the daughter of a clergyman who gave up his ministry to concentrate on scientific interests, flew as a passenger in the Deperdussin in July 1912. She wrote in her book *Memories of Land and Sky* (Methuen, 1928):

> To fly over water is certainly to taste to the full the joy of flight, and when the water is Windermere and the scenery the pick of English Lakeland, which is to many a traveller the pick of the whole world, in its soft intimate loveliness, the result is something not lightly forgotten.

Captain Wavell Wakefield (1898–1983) was Edward Wakefield's nephew, and later 1st Baron Wakefield of Kendal. Wavell Wakefield landed a Sopwith Pup, a British single-seater biplane fighter aircraft, on the deck of HMS *Vindictive* (completed a few weeks before the end of the war; it saw no active service) on 1 November 1918 at Scapa Flow, a body of water in the Orkney Islands, Scotland. Scapa Flow was the main base of the British Grand Fleet, even though it was unfortified. In 1954, he

Gertrude Bacon and Herbert Stanley Adams.
(*Courtesy of the Lakes Flying Company*)

Wavell Wakefield, educated at Sedbergh (public school), 20 miles from Windermere, was an English rugby union player for Harlequins and England, and a Conservative politician.
(*Courtesy of the Lakes Flying Company*)

bought a controlling shareholding in Ullswater 'Steamers', and in doing so saved the company from bankruptcy. He was also instrumental in the preservation of the Ravenglass & Eskdale Railway, west Cumbria.

The unveiling of the Waterbird Plaque on the Windermere and Bowness Civic Society topograph on The Glebe took place on 20 September 2012. Following research into the history of Waterbird and careful design by a dedicated team from the Civic Society, the plaque was manufactured by a local craftsman and mounted on the wall by a local building company.

The wording on the plaque is: 'Waterbird – The first successful British seaplane flight was made on 25th November 1911 by Captain Edward Wakefield's 'Waterbird' from Hill of Oaks to Bowness Bay. Seaplanes and flying-boats were built, repaired and flown on Windermere from 1911–1920 and 1942–1945.'

Today, construction is under way for a new Waterbird – which will be known as Spirit of Wakefield – and, thanks to a recent Defra ruling, the Lake District National Park Authority now has the power to grant exemption orders to Windermere's speed limit (10 nautical miles per hour) because it has to skim the surface of the water before becoming airborne at 30mph. The replica is being built near Lincoln. Some of the original parts, including the rudder bearing the name A.V. Roe & Co., are held by the RAF's museum service. It will be readily interchangeable between being configured as a seaplane or a landplane. (The term seaplane was introduced in 1913 and was a suggestion of Churchill's.)

Rudder bearing the name of A.V. Roe & Co. (*Courtesy of the Lakes Flying Company*)

Celebrating Windermere airfield. (*Courtesy of Ian Stuart Nicholson*)

The following memorial, unveiled on 25 November 2011, celebrates Windermere's role in starting the seaplane industry. It is at the south end of Cockshott Point, a National Trust property, and not far from Hill of Oaks. The inscription reads:

IN MEMORY OF / WINDERMERE I AIRFIELD / OPENED 25.11.1911 / CLOSED 1920 / DEDICATED TO ALL UNITS / AND PERSONNEL BASED HERE / UNVEILED BY KENNETH P. BANNERMAN / DIRECTOR GENERAL ABCT / 25.11.2011.

CHAPTER THREE

The Lakes Flying Company

Edward Wakefield, building on his success, formed the Lakes Flying Company at Hill of Oaks in January 1912, with Lord Lonsdale as patron. It was a timely development as political unrest was brewing in Europe.

The Hill of Oaks site – now a caravan park – became a centre for Admiralty testing and, by the First World War, for the large-scale training of naval pilots whose graduates fought, and all too often died, over the Western and Mediterranean fronts. In 1916, the Northern Aircraft Company's School was taken over by the RNAS but closed in 1917.

John Lankester Parker (1896–1965) gained his first flying experience as a pilot and instructor flying for the Lakes Flying Company, where he flew, first as a pupil and then as an instructor, between 1914 and 1916. His first assignment with Shorts, the first company in the world to make production aircraft, began on 17 October 1916 when he was asked by Horace Short of Shorts to test fly a batch of six Short bombers from the Eastchurch airfield on the Isle of Sheppey, Kent. Between 1918 and his

The Lakes Flying Co. (*Courtesy of the Lakes Flying Company*)

(*Left*) Parker seated in the Satellite at Lympne airfield in the Kent Downs in September 1924 (fur mittens on the wing). (Aeroplane Monthly)

(*Right*) Murray was killed in a flying accident. (*University of Manchester*)

last official flight as chief test pilot on 22 August 1945, he flew every Shorts prototype on its maiden flight. He was awarded the OBE in June 1942.

Donald Stuart Calthorpe Macaskie (1896–1987), from Laleham in Middlesex (actually born in Headingley, Yorkshire), began his training at the Lakes Flying Company in January 1915. He was shot down over the Somme in 1916 when he lost a leg, became a prisoner of war and was repatriated. He died on the Isle of Man. His logbook is at the Imperial War Museum, London.

Flight Sub-Lieutenant Petchell Burtt Murray (1884–1914), educated at Sedbergh, applied on 29 July 1914 for a commission in the RNAS and was gazetted Flight Sub-Lieutenant on 13 September. He was attached to HMS *Pembroke*. On 21 August 1914, at the Lakes Flying Co., he obtained the Royal Aero Club Aviators' Certificate (No. 881), passing the test on the Lakes hydro-biplane.

On 4 November 1914, while training at the Central Flying School, Upavon, Wiltshire, he was killed in a flying accident at Rushall Down on Salisbury Plain. At an inquest into his death, the coroner paid tribute to the excellent work being done by British aviators in France and added that Murray had 'given his life for his country as truly as though he had died in the trenches'. He was buried at Monton Unitarian Chapelyard, Eccles, Lancashire.

Flight Sub-Lieutenant Gerald Meyrick Part (1892–1980) from Stott Park, Newby Bridge at the southern end of Lake Windermere, who was born in Ulverston, went to Trinity College, Cambridge. His training at the Lakes Flying Company began in May 1915. His date of entry into air service was 11 June 1916 and his Royal Aero Club Aviators' Certificate (No. 3433) was obtained on a Maurice Farman biplane at Royal Naval Air Station, Eastbourne on 24 August 1916. He was made Director of Air Organisation IA on 16 April 1918, but had been found permanently unfit for flying (originally admitted to Chatham Hospital for neurasthenia on 15 October 1917) and not suitable for active service. Neurasthenia was described in 1869 as nervous exhaustion and in 1980 as American Nervousness (Americans were said to be particularly prone to neurasthenia).

David Norman Robertson (d.1917) from Pollokshields, Glasgow was a pilot trained at the Lakes Flying Company. He was posted to France where he took off and was never seen again. He was a second lieutenant in the 60th Squadron Royal Flying Corps (RFC), died on 16 April 1917 and is commemorated on the Arras Flying Services Memorial, Pas de Calais, France. He was awarded the Victory and British War medals. A report in *The Scotsman* on 17 September 1917 said:

> Sec. Lt. D. NORMAN ROBERTSON, Royal Flying Corps, missing since 16th April 1917, and now reported killed on that date, was the eldest son of Mr and Mrs David Robertson, 43 Albert Drive, Pollokshields, GLASGOW. He completed his apprenticeship as an engineer with James Howden & Co. (Ltd.), Glasgow, and afterwards entered the Northern Aircraft Hydroplane School at Windermere, where he took his pilot's certificate. Sec. Lt. Robertson was 23 years of age.

On 20 May 1917, two ex-Windermere pupils were officially credited with the first aerial sinking of a German submarine and were both granted the DSC (Distinguished Service Cross). Their names are Flight Sub-Lieutenants Charles Reginald Morrish (1893–1950), RNAS, who was born in Melbourne, and Henry George Boswell (1892–1970), RNAS, who was born in Canada. The following passage is taken from the Royal Air Force Museum. However, other references state that Kapitanleutnant Gustav Buch's mine-laying submarine *UC-36*, which had sunk twenty-four ships, was rammed by the French steamer *Molière* in the English Channel on 21 May 1917 and that Buch (1887–1917), who also commanded *UB-10* (13 August 1916), died on 21 May 1917.

20 May

A flying boat of the Royal Naval Air Service (RNAS) destroys the first hostile submarine to be sunk by an aircraft without any form of assistance. A 'Large America' flying boat flown by Flight Sub-

(*Left*) This photograph of two unknown soldiers shows the difference between the uniforms of the infantry (in this case the King's Own Royal Lancaster Regiment) and the RFC (left).

(*Right*) Charles Reginald Morrish, 1917. (*Courtesy of his family*)

Lieutenant C.R. Morrish, Royal Naval Air Service, on a 'Spider Web' patrol from Felixstowe sighted and attacked the German submarine *UC-36* on the surface near the North Hinder Light Ship.

Destruction of the submarine was confirmed in January 1919.

As an aside, the Laura Ashley Belsfield Hotel at Windermere was used as a Women's Auxiliary Air Force (WAAF) training base during the Second World War.

WAAF officers at the Belsfield (the WAAF was formed in 1939). Their occupations are written on the reverse of the photograph. These include RAF Admin, Catering, Signals, Air-Raid Warning, Intelligence and Code & Cypher. (*Courtesy of the Lakes Flying Company*)

CHAPTER FOUR

Cases Involving Suspected Spies

In September 1914, a rumour held that a German airship was operating from a clandestine base near Grasmere and flying sorties over Westmorland by night. The story was only dispelled after an RFC pilot, Lieutenant Bentfield (Benny) Charles Hucks (1884–1918), flew over the Lake District several times (September/October 1914) and saw nothing but magnificent scenery. He was a regular at Hendon airfield in northwest London, the first British pilot to loop and, later, inventor of the Hucks starter, and searched the Lake District from a Blériot XI monoplane (Hucks died on 7 November 1918, just days before the end of the First World War, of double pneumonia). What Zeppelins could do in Grasmere, either in the way of observation, dropping bombs or landing soldiers, is not easily perceivable. Why were there such rumours at all?

Dr Brett Holman from the University of New England, New South Wales, Australia and author of *The Next War in the Air: Britain's Fear of the Bomber, 1908–1941*, written in 2014, has researched Zeppelin or aeroplane base rumours that sparked official searches: North-East Scotland, Dumfries and Galloway, the south of Ireland and North-West England centred on Cumbria. He told me the following via email:

> What seems to have started that one was some phantom airship sightings at Barrow-in-Furness, near the shipyards and the Vickers airship shed. There were a number of these at the start of the war, and they kept coming in, including some by military personnel that led to incidents where shots were fired. Because there was next to no possibility that these airships could have come from Germany and British origins could be ruled out, it was deduced that they were probably in some secluded spot, and soldiers and police went out and searched or interviewed locals. Hucks' flight was part of that – by this time the suspect area had expanded to cover Derbyshire, Lancashire and Cumberland. Of course, nothing was found,

because there was nothing there – in effect it was an extension of the spy hysteria in the first few months of the war.

Listen out for siren warning

On the night of 19/20 January 1915, two Zeppelins were heading for Humberside but were diverted by strong winds. They found themselves over Norfolk and went on to drop their bombs on King's Lynn and Great Yarmouth, killing four. It served as a forewarning of what was to come. Air-raid precautions were issued in February 1915, signed by Lieutenant Colonel William Fleetwood Nash (1861–1916), Border Regiment (who commanded the Imperial Light Infantry in the Transvaal War and is inscribed on the Carlisle Cemetery Great War Memorial), and the chief constable of Cumberland and Westmorland. These were published merely as a precaution, not in consequence of any apprehension of an imminent raid by sea or land.

Then in March 1915, the *West Cumberland Times* reported: 'Farmers and occupiers of land are urged by the Food Production Department to see their property is insured against damage by aircraft or bombardment if it exceeds £500.' In the same month, the newspaper carried an advert inserted by Cockermouth Urban Council warning of daylight air-raids, asking the public to listen for siren warnings and 'shelter indoors until all clear'. The *Cumberland News* of 11 June 1915 carried a large advert for the British Dominions General Insurance Company. The advert warned 'Your Fire Policy does not cover damage from Acts of War! Zeppelin Raids.' The company then offered a policy covering bomb, shot, shell, fire and explosion damage caused by aircraft.

There were attempts to make a joke of the fear of Zeppelin attacks. On 20 July 1915, a cartoon appeared in the *WG*. A young woman sits upright in bed, and her husband (in a separate single bed) cowers under the blankets. Young wife (at sound of explosion) 'Thomas! Thomas! The Zeppelins are here. Did you lock the front door?' However, in February 1916 an evening service at Langdale Church was changed from 6.30pm to 5.30pm at the wish of the congregation to hold services in daylight and thus minimize the danger of possible Zeppelin raids and a Lighting Restriction Order came into force for the whole of Westmorland in April 1916. In streets, only the lamps considered essential by the police were to remain on. The *WG* of 23 September 1916 reported that the manager of the Red Lion Hotel, Grasmere was summonsed for not having his lit premises darkened as required under the Defence of the Realm Act (DORA). Light from the hotel illuminated trees about 15 yards away. The manager said that the girls must have forgotten to draw the blinds.

Threat from the skies: this fancy dress entry in a Millom, west Cumbria carnival attempted to make a joke of the fear of Zeppelin attacks.

Suspected Russian spy

Among the First World War spies detailed in MI5 files made available in 2014 are Arthur Ransome (1884–1967), who learned how to sail on Coniston, was sent to the Old College prep school in Windermere (closed in 1936), and went on to Rugby School. He was kept on file by MI5 as a suspected Russian spy.

Ransome first caught the attention of the British intelligence services in 1917 while working as a journalist in Russia for the *Daily News* in Fleet Street, a radical newspaper founded in 1846 by Charles Dickens, and the *Manchester Guardian*, known as the *Guardian* since 1959. His job saw him witness the Great October Socialist Revolution in Russia (7–8 November 1917) at first hand, which was led by the Bolsheviks, and he was on friendly terms with many prominent Bolshevik figures. The Bolsheviks ultimately became the Communist Party of the Soviet Union.

Two files that I saw at The National Archives (TNA) document MI5's intense interest in Ransome in the years 1917–20 as he produced propaganda for the Bolsheviks, travelled between Moscow, Stockholm and the UK, and aroused great debate as to whether he was a genuine Bolshevik or was feigning an interest to enable him to continue his journalistic works or to gather information for the British authorities. The files contain details of his relationship with Evgenia Shelepina (1894–1975), Trotsky's former secretary, whom Ransome married in 1924 having played a large part in arranging her emigration from Russia. (Her ashes were placed next to Ransome's at St Paul's churchyard in the small parish of Rusland near Hawkshead.)

The first file at TNA has eight to nine pages and the second sixty-one. The second, covering 1918–19, is full of scraps of reports about Ransome's activities. The initial reports all suggest that he was a genuine supporter of the Bolsheviks: his supposed marriage to Trotsky's secretary is one of the first events reported (in August 1918), and he is described as 'a keen supporter of Trotsky and is himself an ardent Bolshevik.' On his arrival at Stockholm in August 1918, however, it is reported that he had changed his views, though many are unconvinced and one unidentified MI6 officer states that Ransome had named him as a British agent to two Russians. Unsurprisingly, a close watch was kept on Ransome. This contrasts with a description in March 1919 indicating that he was acting for the British authorities in developing close ties with the Bolsheviks: '(Ransome is) not a Bolshevik…his association with the Bolsheviks was begun, and has been continued throughout, at the direct request of responsible British Authorities. He was first asked to get into the closest possible touch with them by Mr Lindley when he was Chargé d'Affaires.' The file continues to gather information on Ransome,

The grave of Arthur and Evgenia Ransome is in St Paul's churchyard, Rusland. Arthur was the celebrated author, but he was also much more. (*Furness Family History Society*)

including from his interview on return to the UK in April 1919. Ransome returned to Russia in 1919 despite the opposition of MI5, after pressure was applied by the *Manchester Guardian*.

There is further correspondence, but tracing Ransome's movements and career at a lower level of detail, in the second file (covering 1918–37). The debate as to his true political sympathies continues and there are reports about his visit to Ceylon and China later in the 1920s. The file closes with a copy of Ransome's passport renewal form in 1937, at which time it was agreed that his name could be removed from the blacklist.

CHAPTER FIVE

Women's Wartime Work

The First World War for most women in South Lakeland meant staying at home waiting for news from the front, desperately scanning casualty lists and struggling to bring up children and look after families single-handed. Food was in short supply, especially in Barrow, where women employed in munitions worked long shifts in the Vickers shell shops. Only the middle and upper classes could afford to work for free. Men were also engaged on munitions work in Barrow, for example John Charles Birbeck (1882–1965), who married Isabel Murphy (1890–1954), a postwoman (1911) of Main Street, Hawkshead at Hawkshead Church on 24 April 1916. Birbeck, born in Ulverston, was rejected by the British army in September 1914 as medically unfit. Details of another man who worked in munitions are on page 104 (Edward Mawson, born in Ambleside).

The VAD provided nurses and orderlies at home and on the fighting fronts and some members were men. VAD Nellie Taylor (1888–1918) is remembered in Grasmere as a casualty of the First World War and is the only woman to be named on the list of the village dead. She was a driver with the 10th Motor Ambulance Convoy. The Motor Ambulance Convoy, established by the Red Cross, was responsible for the transport of wounded men from Regimental Aid Posts to Advanced Dressing Stations and from there to General Hospitals. New weapons such as the machine gun caused unprecedented damage to soldiers' bodies.

Nellie died in France on 27 June 1918. Her body was not repatriated and she is buried at Mont Huon Military Cemetery, France. Grasmere War Memorial is some distance from St Oswald's Church and contains no names. These are placed within the church. Her name appears high up on the Southport, Lancashire war memorial under 'B.R.C.S. Nellie Taylor. Dvr V.A.D'. She is also remembered on a family memorial at Duke Street Cemetery, Southport with her sister Mary who died in 1897, aged 4. It states that Nellie died on active service.

The organ in St Oswald's with a brass dedication plaque was gifted by John Taylor (1861–1945) and his wife Mary in memory of their daughter Nellie. There was a ceremony in memory of Nellie, who was a fine

A time to reflect. The organ in St Oswald's Church was gifted by John Taylor in memory of his daughter Nellie. (*Courtesy of Ian Stuart Nicholson*)

musician so the organ was a very fitting memorial to her, in October 1923 (*WG* of 6 October 1923). The plaque on the organ case of Austrian oak reads:

DEDICATED TO THE / GLORY OF GOD / & IN LOVING MEMORY OF / NELLIE TAYLOR, VAD / OF THE 10TH MOTOR AMBULANCE CONVOY / BRITISH RED CROSS / WHO DIED IN FRANCE JUNE 27TH 1918 / AND WAS INTERRED AT MONT HUON/MILITARY CEMETERY, LE TREPORT / SECOND DAUGHTER OF / JOHN TAYLOR ESQ CBE/AND MRS TAYLOR / OF HELMSIDE, GRASMERE AND / BRYWOOD, BIRKDALE / THIS ORGAN / IS THE GIFT OF HER SORROWING / PARENTS.

The organ was made by James J. Binns of Bramley, Leeds and Messrs T. Wilson & Sons of Grasmere. On 3 August 2014, St Oswald's held an organ recital in memory of Nellie Taylor.

Nellie, who attended Cheltenham Ladies College, was born in Bolton in 1888 and grew up in the well-to-do part of Birkdale, Southport. Her father, who bought Helmside, a country house in Grasmere, in 1897, invented the first hand-portable fire extinguisher which he patented and then entered the automatic sprinkler and alarm business. By the time of the Great War, his business had grown into a large engineering manu-facturers in Manchester that during the war became a major supplier of wartime goods for the country. His prominence in Manchester engi-neering circles led to him becoming chairman of the Lancashire Anti-submarine Committee, a body appointed by the government to find ways of counteracting the effectiveness of the German fleet of submarines. His interest in Grasmere lasted throughout his remaining life. Every New Year's Day at 11.30am, for many years, he gave a brand-new 6d piece to every child in Grasmere who attended a gathering at the Rothay Hotel, together with an orange and a mince pie.

Agnes Mary Fletcher (1885–1971) also served overseas as a VAD nurse during the war. Agnes Mary, whose family owned collieries in the Bolton area and mined the seams under Atherton, Lancashire, was edu-cated at Cheltenham Ladies College and Lady Margaret Hall, Oxford. At the time of the 1911 census, she was living at Crow How, Ambleside, now a guest house (alongside Rydal Farm). In June 1915, she was serving at the No. 16 General Hospital (established February 1915, taken over by the US army) at Le Tréport. She was Men-tioned in Despatches for brave conduct by Field Marshal Douglas Haig, Commander of the BEF during the First World War. She was also recorded as serving at Wimereux and at Genoa in Italy. By February 1919, with the war over, Agnes Mary had returned to England and was working at a military hospital in Weymouth. She was officially demobbed from military hospital service in May 1919. By 1922, she was living with her brother Clement at Atherton, Manchester.

Agnes Mary Fletcher was the only girl out of Katherine and Ralph Fletcher's eight children. (Bolton News)

She died on 18 February 1971 and was buried in Atherton Cemetery.

Lucy Eleanor Jolley (1870–1943) of Lorton in the Northern Lakes had just been appointed matron-in-chief of the Independent Air Force after a brilliant nursing career, according to the *Daily Mirror* of 3 July 1918. Miss Jolley, who received her training at Guy's Hospital, London, was appointed matron of the Royal Southern Hospital, Liverpool on 15 September 1910. The Independent Air Force was a strategic bombing force that was part of the RAF and was used to strike against German railways, aerodromes and industrial centres without co-ordination with the army or navy. Miss Jolley, who had three brothers and one sister, died in Surrey in 1943 (no known children).

The WI have been researching Louisa Mary Holme of Winster as part of the CWGC Living Memory Project. She was born in Ambleside to John, a wood carter, and Mary Holme (née Black) in 1892. She had six siblings, three of whom died in childhood.

Louisa moved to Bournemouth and worked as an assistant dress-maker. Then in the war she joined the QMAAC and became a fore-woman clerk in an overseas hostel in Folkestone from 1917 to 1919. Here she came into contact with injured and sick servicemen returning from the Somme and contracted tuberculosis. She was discharged 'on account of ill health through services rendered' and returned to her family home in Winster where she died on 19 May 1920, aged 28.

On Sunday, 23 October 2016, a service was held at Winster Church and the existing war memorial was re-unveiled. Some forty people gathered around the memorial to hear of Louisa's short life and ultimate sacrifice. A prayer was said and flowers laid at her grave.

Auxiliary hospitals
The patients at auxiliary hospitals were generally less badly wounded than those at other hospitals and they needed to convalesce. In West-morland, the auxiliary hospitals during the First World War were Calgarth Park, Troutbeck Bridge; Stramongate School, Kendal (the first trainload of wounded soldiers from the front arrived in mid-March 1915); St Thomas's Institute, Kendal; Hyning, Milnthorpe; Lowfields, Kirkby Lonsdale; Underley, Kirkby Lonsdale; The Red House, Appleby; Barbon Cottage, Barbon; and Broad Leys, Windermere.

Broad Leys was designed by Charles F.A. Voysey (1857–1941) as a holiday home in 1898 for coal-mine owner Arthur Currer Briggs (1855–1906) of Leeds, whose wife Helen Currer Briggs (née Jones) co-founded the Leeds Children's Holiday Camp at Silverdale for underprivileged children in Leeds. At the outbreak of the First World War, the holiday camp buildings were offered for use as a hospital, a training centre, or a hostel for Belgian refugees. However, none of these offers was taken up and children continued to enjoy their holidays there. Helen Briggs also provided an operating theatre at Beckett's Park Military Hospital, Leeds during the First World War (today part of Leeds Metropolitan University). Mr Briggs, a strict Unitarian who was elected Mayor of Leeds in 1903, died in 1906 at Windermere; Broad Leys is now the Windermere Motor Boat Racing Club.

Joseph Coy Le Fleming Burrow (1888–1967), born in Windermere, the son of landowner and gentleman-farmer Robert Fleming Burrow and Sarah Jane Mackereth, graduated in medicine in 1910. He served during the First World War in the RAMC at Beckett's Park Military Hospital and in Egypt. He was a colourful character, always immaculately dressed, and with great charm. He was one of the early owners of a Bentley and hunted with the Bramham Moor Hounds, Yorkshire.

Private Ernest Beach (1895–1915), 2nd East Yorkshire Regiment, was among a batch of wounded brought to Windermere in March 1915. Beach, of Lime Street, Hull, died on 21 March 1915 in Westmorland County Hospital, Kendal, from wounds. He was educated at Charterhouse School, Hull, a Victorian board school built in 1881 that became a secondary school in 1950. Prior to the outbreak of war, he worked in the timber industry. He enlisted on 2 September 1914 and had only been at the Front for eleven days when he was wounded while on guard by shrapnel. He is buried at Hull (Hedon Road) Cemetery. Westmorland County Hospital (opened 1908) was at the top of Captain French Lane in Central Kendal. It closed in 1990 when the Westmorland General was built on a greenfield site on the A65 on the outskirts of town.

The following is a list of ladies whose homes were in the parish of St Martin's, Windermere who were VADs (members of the Voluntary Aid Detachment during the First World War; in parentheses the hospitals in which they served): Helen Maroh Bownass (b.1884) (Calgarth) of Lattimers, Windermere in 1911; Hilda Burrill (b.1898) (Calgarth and Broad Leys); Elsie Birkett (b.1893) (Liverpool) who worked as a housemaid at Bank House, Windermere in 1911; Lady Bromley-Wilson, Alice Dobson (b.1873) (Calgarth) of Knott End, Windermere in 1911; M. Fiern (Calgarth and Manchester); Margaret Alice Geddes (b.1866) (Calgarth); Betty Johnson (Broad Leys); Barbara Johnson (France); Elizabeth Bateman Johnson (b.1884) (Calgarth) of Crescent Road, Windermere in 1911; Annie Leece (Broad Leys); Ada Nicholson (b.1879) (Calgarth); Nellie Pattinson (PC Relief Council, London); Annie Tomlinson (Calgarth and Oxford); Amelia Tomlinson (Calgarth and Oxford); Phyllis Tweedale (1892–1981) (Broad Leys); and Madge Tweedale (PC Relief Council, London).

Mrs Oswald Hedley of Briery Close, Ambleside helped to organize the conversion of their property at Calgarth Park to a hospital for wounded Belgian and British officers. She died in March 1916. After the war, the hospital was re-opened as the Ethel Hedley Orthopaedic Hospital for Children in her memory. As an aside, a group of Jewish children who came to be known as the Windermere Boys were granted refuge at the Calgarth estate in 1945.

A Child Holocaust Survivors Tree was planted on 14 August 2015 by Ben Helfgott MBE, Honorary President of the Holocaust Memorial Day Trust, and dedicated by him on 27 January 2017. It was presented to commemorate the seventieth anniversary of his arrival at this site in the summer of 1945. He came as part of a group of 300 orphaned Jewish child Holocaust survivors who came to the Lake District directly from the concentration camps. The children stayed in hostels located on the Calgarth Estate, which stood on this site between 1942 and 1964. It was here that they began to rebuild their shattered lives. This tree was originally grown from an acorn and nurtured in Cumbria by Trevor Avery BEM, Director of the Lake District Holocaust Project. The acorn had been gathered from the foot of a tree that still stands today at the place of huge sorrow near Oświęcim in Poland. Oświęcim translates to 'Auschwitz' in German and was so named by the Nazi German occupiers in the Second World War. The Auschwitz concentration camp complex was the largest of its kind established by the Nazi regime.

Lady Elizabeth Ann Bromley-Wilson (1867–1936) became a Dame after re-marriage in London on 16 December 1916 and died at her home – Dallam Tower, Milnthorpe, a Grade I listed country house – in 1936. Her first husband was Major Godfrey Armitage (1871–1913) who was in the 3rd Battalion Lancashire Fusiliers at the time of his death. He died at Nab Wood, Windermere. He had been instructor of musketry (firearms) to the 5th Battalion Lancashire Fusiliers, Militia Infantry at Bury, Lancashire for more than six years and fought with the 5th Battalion Lancashire Fusiliers at the Battle of Spion Kop (23–24 January 1900) in the Boer War. There is a memorial plaque to him, the Armitage Plaque, at St Martin's, Windermere. Her new husband had changed his name from Bromley to Bromley-Wilson some time previously by Royal Decree. The owners of Dallam Tower historically had been Wilsons, so perhaps he inherited it and the name change was a condition of inheritance.

A nurse tells her story

In April 1915, newly-trained VADs Dorothea Mary Lynette Crewdson (1887–1919) and her best friend Christie received instructions to leave for Le Tréport hospital in northern France (she worked in three hospitals). Dorothea, whose family came from Westmorland and whose cousins still lived in Windermere, began writing diaries. 'Who knows how long we shall really be out here? Seems a good chance from all reports of the campaigns being ended before winter but all is uncertain,' she said. Dorothea, from Nottingham, described the day-to-day realities and frustrations of nursing near the front line of the battlefields, or the pleasure of a beautiful sunset, or a trip 'joy-riding' in the French

Windermere links: Dorothea's diaries, edited by her nephew Richard Crewdson, were
deposited with the Imperial War Museum after her brother Alastair's death.
(*The Woodland Trust*)

countryside on one of her precious days off, or flirtations with the
doctors. One day she might be gossiping about her fellow nurses, or
confessing to writing her diary while on shift on the ward, or illustrating
the scene of the tents collapsing around them on a windy night in one of
her vivid sketches. She received the Military Medal for her actions in
1918. According to the *London Gazette* of 30 July 1918, it was for
gallantry and devotion to duty during an enemy air-raid. Although herself wounded, she remained on duty and assisted in dressing the wounds
of patients. She died on 12 March 1919, on active service, from peri-
tonitis (this occurs when the thin layer of tissue lining the abdomen
becomes infected with bacteria or fungi), and was buried at Étaples
Military Cemetery. Her father Henry Crewdson (1852–1924) was born
in Kendal and educated at Windermere College. Henry Crewdson
Broadwick (1874–1956), in the family, was born in High Wray Bank,
Ambleside and died in Windermere. Another family member, Reverend
George Crewdson (1840–1920), worked as vicar of St Mary's, Windermere from 1893 to 1910.

The *WG* of 30 January 1915 reported that Private Stephen Moffat
(1883–1939), Coldstream Guards, of Grasmere was returned from the

front to a VAD hospital in England suffering from rheumatism. He said that where he had come from was the worst place in the whole line. They were up to their knees in mud. They had had a fierce battle on 28 December 1914. There were hundreds of dead lying about that could not be buried as it was too dangerous to try. At the outbreak of the First World War, Coldstreamers were among the first British regiments to arrive in France. At the First Battle of Ypres (19 October to 22 November 1914), the 1st Battalion (1/CG) was virtually annihilated. By 1 November it was down to 150 men and the lieutenant quartermaster.

WAAC

The Women's Army Auxiliary Corps (WAAC), re-named the Queen Mary's Auxiliary Army Corps (QMAAC) in April 1918, was formed in 1917. Approximately 57,000 women joined the WAAC, performing non-combatant roles such as clerical and mechanical work. Most of these served within the UK. The Corps was disbanded in 1921.

Mary Baisbrown Biddle (1885–1968), the eldest daughter of Richard and Agnes Baisbrown (née Thompson), was born in Grasmere and lived in College Road, Grasmere at the start of the First World War. According to photographic evidence, she joined the WAAC. After the Second World War, she married Percy Biddle in the London area and returned to Grasmere in the early 1960s a widow, living at High Fieldside.

Mary Baisbrown's younger sister Nellie Baisbrown (1897–1970) also joined the WAAC. Family member Carrie Taylor told me that Nellie won an OBE. She said:

> But it doesn't state exactly what it was for. Being of the lower class ranks, it was not a full-blown OBE. The *London Gazette* of 23 January 1929 states the Medal of the Most Excellent Order of the British Empire (Military Division). Only the great and the good got proper gongs.

Family member Alan who lives in Bromley, Kent told me about meeting Mary. He said:

> My gut reaction is that both sisters (Mary and Nellie) signed up at a local unit, transferred to London. As they were already well versed in 'service', they were put into the officers' mess. We believe that Nellie saw service in France at one point. But there are little or no surviving records at The National Archives in Kew.

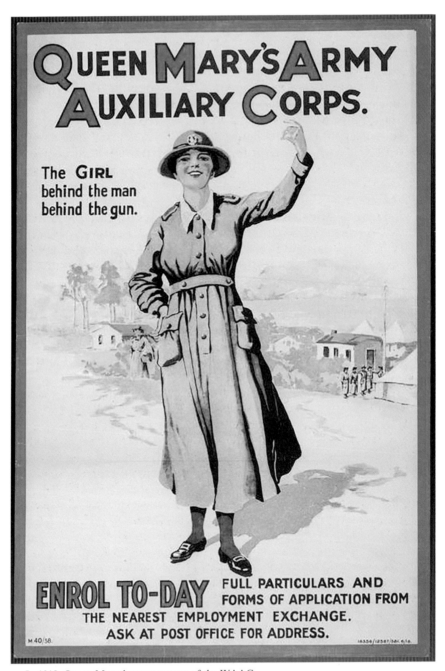

In 1918, Queen Mary became patron of the WAAC.

After the war, Nellie was a founder member of the women's section of the British Legion in Grasmere. Their sister Amy Baisbrown (1892–1981), who lived at College Street, Grasmere (1911 census), was a housemaid by trade, helping in B&Bs such as Miss Winnie Borwick's before the First World War. She took up the job of postwoman throughout Grasmere valley during the war. Often bringing very sad tidings, she delivered all the post on foot in order to conserve fuel.

The homes of Lily Atkinson (WAAC), L. Adams (WAAC) and H. Willshaw (WAAC) were in the parish of St Martin's. WAAC member Annie Maude Ellwood (1896–1991), born in Staveley, wrote to the National Service Department in London in February 1917 offering herself for service abroad in response to a government advertisement in the *Yorkshire Post*. Her original application form shows that she had worked as a clerk for the previous nine months. After passing a medical examination, she enrolled as a clerk in the WAAC on 8 May 1917. Within the space of three weeks she had departed for France where she remained – except for periods of leave – for the next two years. According to her casualty form (active service), she worked in clerical posts at various British army transport depots, most notably in Abbeville. She does not appear to have left the military transport depot at Abbeville until May 1919, after which she was given another clerical posting at Calais. Following a two-week period of sick leave in England in July, she was finally discharged from the QMAAC in October 1919.

Evelyn May Burns (b.1900), who was born in Windermere, was 18 and living at Chorley, Lancashire when she enlisted in the WAAC in 1918. A letter (dated March 1939) addressed to Mrs E.H. Higham of Levis Garth, Haverthwaite, held at TNA, states that in order to have qualified for the award of the Great War Medal, Evelyn should have served outside the UK between August 1914 and 18 November 1918. Evelyn, who was 5ft 1in, was stationed at Newport, south-east Wales, Chadderton, 1 mile west of Oldham and Conwy on the north coast of Wales. Mary Agnes Palmer (b.1893) of Rose Cottage, Great Langdale, enrolled in the WAAC on 3 September 1918. Annie Elizabeth Barker (b.1894) of 2 The Glen, Haverthwaite, enrolled in the WAAC on 20 April 1917. She worked as a clerk, left Southampton on 12 June 1917 and disembarked at Le Havre on the following day. She was issued a casualty form on active service and left Rouen (Camp VI) on 2 June 1919. The existing war memorial at Winster, Windermere (IWM ref. 4242) was re-unveiled on 23 October 2016 at a service to the seven servicemen and of the parish and Louise Mary Holme (1892–1920) of Winster. Some forty people gathered around the memorial to hear of her short life and sacrifice. A prayer was said and flowers laid at her grave.

The WI has been researching her as part of the CWGC Living Memory Project. She was born in Ambleside to John (a wood carter) and Mary Holme (née Black) in 1892. She had six siblings, but three of those died in childhood. She moved to Bournemouth and worked as an assistant dressmaker. In the war, she joined the QMAAC and became a forewoman clerk in an overseas hostel in Folkestone from 1917 to 1919. Here, she came into contact with injured servicemen returning to the Somme and contracted TB. She was discharged 'on account of ill health through services rendered' and returned to her family home (Winster) where she died on 19 May 1920, aged 28.

Women's work on the land
The function of the War Agricultural Executive Committees ('War Ags') – established in autumn 1915 and appointed by each county council – was to organize the supply of agricultural labour, increase production of food, obtain information about the requirements and supply of agricultural implements, machinery, fertilisers and foodstuffs, and to assist and advise landowners, farms and labourers and inform the Board of Agriculture of difficulties. The Westmorland County War Agricultural Committee held its first meeting on 9 October 1915. G.H. Pattinson was joint chairman. Mr E.H. Jackson was a member of the committee for Windermere and E.D. McNaughtan for Ambleside. Westmorland County War Agricultural Committee was told at its meeting in Kendal in January 1916 that between thirty and forty women in the county not usually engaged in farm work had put their names forward as willing to undertake it. This was not a large total but was sufficient to warrant an experiment.

The Department of Agriculture set up the Women's Branch of the Labour Committee with Dame Meriel Talbot (1866–1956) as director. She formed the Women's National Land Services Corps in 1915. When 1917 came, many women and girls responded to the call of 'back to the land'. Thus the Women's Land Army (WLA) was formed to provide the mobile workforce needed to supplement the reduced number of male workers on the land and to provide the nation with its vital food supplies. The demand for recruits was made either through the press or at open-air rallies and meetings in London and throughout the country. By 1918, there were 23,000 Land Girls.

The WLA was disbanded in 1919. Some members continued on the land, some falling in love with and marrying farmers or becoming farmers themselves. This romanticized version was perhaps appropriate in the immediacy of the return to peace.

CHAPTER SIX

Refugees in South Lakeland

In Ulverston, twenty-four refugees arrived at Lund Hall on 31 September 1914, mainly of the artisan class from Leuven, 16 miles east of Brussels in Belgium. One of the four women was English: a Mrs Turney who had been living between Malines, Belgium and Brussels, and had to abandon her house when she was in the middle of cooking the evening meal.

From the *WG* of various dates, it can be established that the first arrivals in Kendal were on 9 October 1914, when twenty-nine arrived. A crowd of an estimated 3,000 people had assembled to give them a rousing reception. They had been travelling for several weeks via Nieuport (Belgium), Ostend (Belgium), Folkestone in Kent, Edmonton in north London and Liverpool. They were from Aerschot, Malines and Rillaert and comprised the following: a horseman, his wife and daughter; a painter (45), his wife and five children aged 14, 11, 7, 4 and 1; a widow cane chair seat-maker with her own three children aged 8, 6 and 2, also with three girls aged 18, 18 and 12 and a boy aged 12 from three families, but all four orphaned; a knife-maker aged 63 from Aerschot with his wife and two children aged 12 and 17; and a sawyer with his wife and five daughters aged between 3 months and 14 years.

They were looked after in four hostels under the banner name 'Belgian Settlement for Kendal and District' with the treasurer Isaac Braithwaite; each was looked after by a matron and a stores/housekeeping committee. The hostels were called Prospect, Castle Mount, Holly Croft and Silverhow (all on Kendal Green). The driving force behind the settlement was Arthur William Simpson (1857–1922), the head of a wood-carving business in Kendal, and his wife Jane Simpson (née Davidson) (1861–1950), both Quakers. The Simpsons had a daughter Hilda (b.1893) who worked as a home assistant in 1911. Jane Simpson, who was born in Monaghan, Ireland, was awarded the Medaille de la Reine Elisabeth, a Belgian decoration created by royal decree on 15 September 1915 to recognize exceptional services to Belgium in the relief of the suffering of its citizens during the First World War. Cumbria is the birthplace of the Quakers (the Religious Society of Friends). Young Quakers set up the Friends' Ambulance Unit (FAU) that operated from 1914 to 1919. The hamlet of Colthouse near Hawkshead has one of the oldest Quaker Meeting Houses, erected in 1688. A separate Quaker burial ground is nearby, which pre-dates this building.

The refugees on 9 October 1914 were followed on 16 October 1914 by a further forty-four. Of the seventy-three now in the town, thirteen were men, twenty-two women and thirty-eight children. All were Roman Catholic and all the children attended the Catholic School. There were twelve from three generations of one family from Liege, Malines and Antwerp.

Among the new arrivals were a sabot-maker aged 21; a machinist aged 62; a boot-maker aged 55; a mechanic aged 22; two dock labourers aged 20 and 54; a ship's painter aged 37; a hairdresser aged 23; a diamond-cutter aged 28; a clerk aged 24; and an upholsterer aged 32. The clerk, Monsieur Wery Camille, had served in the 34th Regiment of the Belgian army at Liege. One of the women had her husband and two of her sons as prisoners of the Germans with the other four sons missing,

From Westmorland list of FAU members. (*Courtesy of Cyril Pearce*)

84   85

WESTMORLAND.

ADDISON, E.	Bridge End, Stainton, Kendal	Nov./15—Jan./19, D, AT 17, V.
ALLEN, S. R.	Sunnyholme, Wattsfield, Kendal	Sept./16—Feb./19, GS.
BOWKER, O.	8, Ash Meadows, Kendal	May/16—Feb./19, KG, D.
CARTER, J. N.	8, Greenside, Kendal	July/16—Jan./19, GS.
GAWITH, S. H.	Runswick, Kentrigg, Kendal	June/16—Feb./19, KG, D.
HALL, J.	Low Park House, Preston Richard, nr. Kendal	July/18—Dec./18, GS.
HOLMES, F.	32, Romney Rd., Kendal	Jan./17—Feb./19, GS.
HOLMES, G.	32, Romney Rd., Kendal	Jan./17—Feb./19, GS.
INGHAM, G. F.	Holly Bank, Arnside	Nov./17—Feb./19, GS.
JEFFERYS, Miss B.	Castle Green, Kendal	Dec./16—Dec./18, D.
JEFFERYS, G.	Castle Green, Kendal	July/16—Feb./19, D, SSA 13.
JONES, D. A.	126, Highgate, Kendal	June/16—Jan./19, KG, D.
JONES, E.	Harwood Dale, Kendal	June/17—Jan./19, D, Com.
KIDD, T. H.	Pembroke St., Appleby	June/17—Jan./19, GS.
KING, A. J.	Elleray, Windermere	Com.
KING, J. F. O.	Elleray, Windermere	Sept./14—May/15, D.
KING, P. F.	Elleray, Windermere	Jan./16—Feb./19, D, SSA 19.
LITTLE, J. R.	Applethwaite Lodge, Windermere	Sept./14—Mar./19, L, Com.
LITTLE, Mrs. J. R.	Applethwaite Lodge,	Sept./14—Mar./19, L.
LONG, D. S.	Scarfoot, Skelsmergh, Kendal	Jan./16—Dec./18, D, SSA 13, U.
O'BRIEN, T. H.	Wraysholme, Ambleside	Oct./15—Dec./18, D, GS.
SIMPSON, R. B.	Little Holme, Kendal	Sept./14—Jan./15, D.
TATHAM, G. W.	8, Nether Street, Kendal	May/18—Feb./19, GS.
WILSON, C. B.	5, Bankfield, Kendal	Aug./16—Dec./18, GS.

CUMBERLAND.

Alsop, H. F. ...	The Ruddings, Cockermouth	Nov./15—Feb./19, AT 17.
Altham, W. R....	Brunswick Hall, Penrith	Feb./16—Feb./19, SG, D.
Attrill, A. J. ...	c/o Kerr & Sons, Ltd., 8, Corn Market, Penrith	June/16—Dec./18, Y, AT 17, AT 5, D, SG, GS.
Brockbank, W.	Heathfield, Brayton, Carlisle	Jan./16—Aug./15, D.
Carr, W. R. ...	Wigton Hall, Wigton ...	Aug./15—Feb./19, D, AT 16, SSA 14.
Collins, P. F. ...	Mayo St., Cockermouth	Jan./16—Mar./19, D.
Dixon, N. ...	79, Senhouse St., Maryport.	Feb./16—Dec./18, Y.
Hall, C. E. ...	52, Vale View, Harrington.	Aug./16—Dec./18, GS.
Hall, J. H. ...	Waverton, Wigton ...	Jan./15—Oct./15, D.
Hall, Richard W.	5, Morland Place, Cockermouth	Aug./16—Dec./18, GC, U.
Hinde, J. D. ...	Croft House, Brigham, Cockermouth	Dec./15—Feb./19, D, AT 11.
Hutchinson, M. S.	8, Newby West, Carlisle	May/16—Feb./19, V.
Jackson, W. R....	Green Lane House, Brampton	May/16—Feb./19, D, AT 16.
Leck, A. S. ...	36, Musgrave St., Penrith	Apl./16—Dec./18, Y.
Lester, A. L. ...	Forest Mount, Penrith ...	Sept./15—Mar./19, Y, D.
Mandale, M. E.	Woodhall Farm, Cockermouth	Nov./17—Dec./18, GS,
Marshall, C. E.	Derwent Island, Keswick	Oct./15—Feb./19 D, SSA 13.
Park, T. ...	Underwood, Mosser, Cockermouth	June/16—Feb./19, KG, D.
Pask, A. F. ...	Barrow House, Keswick	Aug./16—Dec./18, GS.
Patrickson, J. N.	Henry Street, Cockermouth	July/16—Dec./18, Y, GS.
Peile, J. A. ...	Parkgate Hall, Wigton...	Jan./15—June/15, D.
Peile, T. M. ...	Parkgate Hall, Wigton...	June/16—Jan./19, KG, D.

Robertson, R....	5, Arthur Terrace, Penrith	Sept./16—Nov./18, GS.
Ward, Walter	Heathfield, Brayton, Carlisle	June/16—Feb./19, GS.

From Cumberland list of FAU members. (*Courtesy of Cyril Pearce*)

and two of her three daughters were still in London, the family having become separated in the confusion.

On 22 October 1914 there was a refugee family at Rothay Manor, Ambleside, a country house hotel. Joseph Burseniers (a master builder), his wife Louise, and son Marcel Abta with his wife of three months, Juliette, had arrived via the Ostend to Folkestone boat. There is also reference to refugees accommodated at Ellerthwaite Lodge B&B in Windermere.

On 5 November 1914, there is reference to the house Highfield at Hawkshead being made available for a family but doubt as to whether a licence would be granted as Hawkshead was a restricted area (It has not been possible to establish why it was a restricted area, i.e. an area that could only be entered by authorized people. As far as is known, information on restricted areas was never published). Also on 5 November, a Belgian family arrived at Finsthwaite, a small village near the Furness Fells and Windermere that has Stott Park Bobbin Mill. The vicar met them at a station and they were conveyed to the new residence in a conveyance flying the Belgian flag.

On 10 November 1914, an electrician, his wife and four children were moved to a bungalow that had been made available at Newby Bridge. He had been a corporal in the Belgian army. On 16 November 1914, nine wounded Belgian soldiers arrived at Calgarth Park, Windermere, followed by five more two days later. A day or two after Christmas, these same wounded were called back to the realities of war.

Low Nook on Rydal Road, Ambleside was made available. Fifteen refugees arrived there on 16 November 1914 and five more two days later. When the Belgian refugees first occupied Low Nook, there was among them an elderly lady with three grandchildren whose mother had become separated from them. Her whereabouts was not known. On 20 February 1915, she arrived at Low Nook and the joy of meeting her family again can well be imagined.

The *WG* of 12 December 1914 reported on a dance in a parish near Ambleside in aid of the local Belgian refugees. The vicar scolded his flock for the inequity in doing such a thing, even for a charitable objective, at a time when so many of their brethren were shivering and perishing in the trenches. He said it was a disgrace.

A group of wounded Belgians being cared for at Calgarth Park. Special parties were arranged for wounded Belgian soldiers and refugees at Calgarth Park and for refugees at Holly Croft and Prospect House, Kendal. (Westmorland Gazette)

An article in the *Penrith Observer* on 2 March 1915 reported on a scheme devised by James Watt to provide work on farms for Belgian refugees. It had come to an end. The paper said:

> An enormous majority of the men who have come to Great Britain from Belgium seem to have been accustomed to occupations other than agriculture. It would be as unreasonable to expect these to be able to adapt themselves to rural occupations as it would be to suppose that Lancashire operatives could do a similar emergency turn to the work of a Cumberland fellside farm.

The first ship to repatriate the Belgian refugees from Scotland and the Northern Counties sailed from Grimsby on 12 December 1918 for Antwerp. In the early stages, all costs were met by the British government.

On 9 February 1919, Monsieur Jaen Claes (aged 66) attempted to murder his 71-year-old wife at their home – Holly How, Coniston – and then killed himself by hanging. He was from Malines, where he had run a brass founding business. He had been in Coniston since 20 October 1914 and had been due to return to Belgium shortly but was said to have become depressed on hearing that his business and machinery had been totally destroyed in the war. He is buried in St Andrew's churchyard, Coniston.

A formal letter of thanks for the hospitality of the UK to the refugees was sent in August 1919 from His Excellency Monsieur le Baron de Brocqueville, Minister of the Interior for Belgium. It is reproduced on page three of the *Millom Gazette* dated 15 August 1919. The Millom Belgian refugee population was by far the largest and the story is also comprehensively told in the *Millom Gazette*. By the end of 1914, Millom had a population of well under 10,000 but still managed to squeeze in 1,000 Belgians. According to the *WG* of 1 November 1919, at the peak there had been around 100 refugees in Windermere.

CHAPTER SEVEN

Help on the Home Front

For ordinary people at home in unusual times, weddings and 'boon' clips – when neighbours and friends gathered at a farm to shear the sheep (largely a thing of the past) – continued. On the other hand, women were steadily knitting and sewing since their men left and rationing was implemented. Within the first month of the war, Hawkshead parish council started a committee for relief work and a rifle club for those over 16 years of age. The *Whitehaven News* reported on 12 November 1914 that the Grasmere Relief Committee had sent eighty pairs of socks and forty belts to the Red Cross. It also reported that the women of Graythwaite had sent ten flannel shirts, nineteen hospital shirts, eleven pairs of socks, a woollen cap and a parcel of useful articles to the Lancashire Fusiliers.

On 1 February 1915, a second instalment of £10 was sent from the collecting boxes of Windermere in support of the Lake Windermere Fund for the upkeep of the motor ambulances at the front. The *WG* of 6 February 1915 reported on the Heathwaite Mission Sewing Meeting at Windermere. So far they had sent sixty-nine pairs of socks, twelve belts, twenty-four mufflers, five helmets, twenty-one pairs of mittens, soap, stationery, pencils, peppermints, combs, buttons and boxes of ointments. On 20 February 1915, a letter was published in the *WG* asking for readers to send old kid, leather or suede gloves to Mrs Stock of Fisher Beck, Ambleside. They were to be used for making waistcoats for the soldiers, keeping out the cold wind more effectively than wool. On 3 April 1915, Ambleside had so far sent 2,066 eggs to the national egg collection. The *WG* of 12 June 1915 reported that St Mary's Infants School, Windermere had collected 15s.4d for comforts for soldiers and sailors.

The following is an extract from *Parish News, June 1915* (Windermere St Mary's), entitled 'Tubs for Tommies':

We stated in last month's magazine that £50 had been collected from parishioners and their friends in order to purchase Baths with a Stove for every five baths, for the Soldiers at the Front. We stated, that with this £50, five stoves and twenty-five Baths had been sent out to the Troops. Since the issue of the last Magazine, four more stoves and twenty more baths have been sent at a cost of £40. Every £10 provides one stove and five baths, and they give 100 men a bath daily, and in addition 10 gallons of water for the men to use in making tea, instead of boiling water for tea in their own greasy pans ... It is considered that they will assist in keeping down Typhus Fever, we appeal for more contributions of 5s (less or more) which may be sent to Miss Makant, Old Fallbarrow (Windermere), or to The Rector.

August 1915

Mary Augusta Ward was born in Tasmania, Australia. Her uncle was the poet Matthew Arnold (1822–88). Her sister Julia married Leonard Huxley, the son of Thomas Huxley, and their sons were Julian and Aldous Huxley (1894–1963), the latter best known for his novels including *Brave New World* set in a dystopian London. The Arnolds and the Huxleys were an important influence on British intellectual life.

She sent Wordsworth's grandson, Gordon Graham Wordsworth (1860–1935), an extract from her writing *Wordsworth's Valley in War-Time* during the first years of the war, which was later included in the *Book of the Homeless* by American novelist Edith Wharton (1862–1937) in 1916 (pp. 151–5). Ward wrote:

> 8 August 1915. It is now four days since, in this village of Grasmere, at my feet, we attended one of those anniversary meetings, marking the first completed year of this appalling war, which were being called on that night over the length and breadth of England. Our meeting was held in the village schoolroom: the farmers, trades-men, inn-keeper and summer visitors of Grasmere were present, and we passed the resolution which all England was passing at the same moment, pledging ourselves, separately and collectively, to help the war and continue the war, till the purposes of England were attained, by the liberation of Belgium and northern France, the chastisement of Germany.
>
> And I stand to-night on this lovely mountain-side, looking out upon the harvest fields of another August, and soon another even-ing newspaper sent up from the village below will bring the latest list of our dead and our maimed.

Every man from Grasmere got a Christmas present of two pairs of socks, Ward wrote in August 1915:

Two sisters, washerwomen, and hard worked, made a pair each, in four consecutive weeks, getting up at four in the morning to knit. Day after day, women from the village have gone up to the fells to gather the absorbent sphagnum moss, which they dry and clean, and send to a manufacturing chemist to be prepared for hospital use. Half a ton of feather-weight moss has been collected and cleaned by women and school-children. One old woman who could not give money gathered the tufts of wool which the sheep leave behind them on the brambles and fern, washed them, and made them into the little pillows which prop wounded limbs in hospital.

The cottages and farms send eggs every week to the wounded in France. The school-children also bring fifty a week. One woman, whose main resource was her fowls, offered twelve eggs a week; which meant starving herself. And all the time, two pence, three pence, six pence a week was being collected by the people themselves, from the poorest homes, towards the support of the Belgian colony in the neighbouring village of Ambleside.

Mary Wilkinson, a schoolgirl of Grasmere, received a letter from a wounded soldier thanking her for eggs, as reported by the *WG* on 21 August 1915. Driver B. Nicholson, Royal Field Artillery, in hospital at Aldershot, Hampshire wrote:

Having received one of your eggs for breakfast this morning, I take the liberty of writing to you to tell you of my big accident. We were riding along at Aldershot with big guns and wagons when some sixty of our horses took fright. We could not hold them for love or money. I was centre driver on a six-horse team. We were descending the very steep hill called Gunhill and the wagons had six or seven tons on them. In the runaway the horses knocked down eight lamp posts and caused an explosion. I rode about a hundred yards when I was trampled on by my horse and kicked in the head, which knocked me unconscious. Then the wagon passed over my leg and broke it. I have a compound fracture and have had five operations. In the last one they put a silver plate in my leg with nine gold screws into the bone. I have been a raving maniac with the pain and am afraid, Mary I shall never be able to ride another horse. I am 24 years old.

In September 1915, there was egg-collecting in Finsthwaite and in Seathwaite. There was further egg-collecting in Finsthwaite in December 1916. Since April 1915, 6,682 had been collected. During the First World War, the older girls of Langdale knitted socks that were sent to the Red

Cross. The following is taken from *Cumbria Within Living Memory*, Cumbria Federation of Women's Institutes (1994): 'Our vicar gave us permission to take our knitting to church (Holy Trinity, Great Langdale) and knit during the sermon. We had concerts at school to get cash to pay for the wool.'

Sandbags

There was a Parochial Working Party, meeting once a week from August 1914 to May 1919, organized by Mrs Nurse and Miss Makant. It made and sent off more than 9,000 articles of clothing to the troops and 19,000 sandbags to France. Sandbags were a vital part of the trenches. They stopped the sides from collapsing and provided protection from bullets and shell blasts. The Windermere boatmen assisted with the sandbags. They used their sail-making skills to sew up sandbags to War Office regulations at a cost of 4d per bag. Accompanying the photograph on the next page, in the *WG* on 21 August 1915, was an associated poem:

> We are all sewing bags for sand,
> To send out to that stricken land,
> Where our brave fighters at the Front,
> So fearlessly now bear the brunt.

The *Whitehaven News* reported on 9 December 1915 that 450 sand-bags had been made in Ambleside. Also a whist drive was held at Hawkshead in aid of soldiers' Christmas presents. The *WG* reported on 1 January 1916 that the offerings at Grasmere on Christmas Day were for the Sunday schools and starving Belgians. Envelopes were also left at every house to be passed round at the Christmas dinner and the sums so contributed were also for the Belgian National Relief Fund. The *WG* said:

> Miss H. Sumner took a party of carol singers round the village on one or two evenings previous to Christmas Day. Special subscriptions were given with the object of providing Grasmere men with extra Christmas gifts in the form of pipes, tobacco, and sweets, in addition to woollen comforts, and sixty-three parcels were sent. Twenty-eight to France, fourteen to the Mediterranean, twenty-one to men in England, and six smaller parcels were also sent to men who have been discharged. Each parcel contained a pipe, and one packet each of shag, twist, cigarettes, and toffee, and three woollen garments. Mr and Mrs Hedley presented a plum pudding to every family in the village which had one of their number fighting for their country.

Sandbag-making at Windermere. (*Museum of Lakeland Life and Industry*)

Cigarettes were given out at the port of Le Havre to wounded British and French soldiers after the Battle of the Marne. Cigarettes, known as 'fags', 'gaspers' or 'Woodbines' were not then considered a grave risk to health but an essential for many soldiers.

On 28 March 1916, the Finsthwaite War Working Party forwarded to the War Hospital Supplies Depot at Barrow twenty shirts and forty-eight pairs of socks. On 11 April 1916, a postal order for 12s was sent to each of the nineteen scholars of Hawkshead on active service out of the net profit of £11.10s.8d realized by the schoolchildren's concert at Hawkshead.

The *WG* on 15 April 1916 reported that the Grasmere Girls' Friendly Society had held a bring-and-buy sale in support of a diocese effort to raise funds for a Church Army hut for the use of soldiers at the front. More than 230 people attended and a net profit of £28.10s was achieved. A public meeting was held at Dale Lodge Hotel, Grasmere on Monday, 15 January 1917, to promote the formation of a Volunteer Training Corps. A further meeting about volunteers was held and reported in the *WG* on 3 March 1917. Sixty men were eligible as volunteers. In August 1917, Hawkshead soldiers on leave made use of transport provided by the Lake District Soldiers and Sailors Arrival Society.

The Grasmere Red Cross Society during the past week had sent every soldier and sailor belonging to Grasmere a parcel containing socks, tobacco, a pipe, cigarettes and toffee, the *WG* reported on 16 December 1916. The sum of £1.4s was being devoted each month for parcels of food to be sent to the four prisoners of war. In January 1917, Penny Bridge schoolchildren knitted for soldiers. A patriotic entertainment in aid of soldiers' comforts was held in Haverthwaite in December 1917.

In October 1918, there was a request in the Ambleside/Brathay/ Hawkshead combined parish magazine for nut shells and plum stones for use in making munitions. This is not a tall story, as the items in question contained essential ingredients that were in short supply in wartime. Similarly, during the Great War children were asked to collect great quantities of conkers for their acetone content, also for use in munitions.

The piece of hessian (sacking) has a label addressed to Private Thomas Walker, 9th Battalion, King's Own Royal Lancaster Regiment, Prisoner of War, Bulgaria. Private Walker was listed as missing in January 1916. The parcel contained 'food' and is dated 24 September 1918. This item was found in the upholstery of a chair and donated to the King's Own Royal Regiment Museum, Lancaster in 1979 by a lady in Windermere. The hessian had been re-used in the manufacture of the chair.

Boy Scouts and the war

Children found their own way of contributing during the Great War. The 1st Windermere Troop Boy Scouts rallied at Windermere on 24 May 1915, Whit Monday, and embarked for Fell Foot, their old camping ground, at the lower end of the lake. Here they entertained the soldiers from Calgarth Park auxiliary hospital for the afternoon.

The *WG* of 11 September 1915 reported that nearly 200 Boy Scouts from fifteen Westmorland troops were inspected at Windermere by General Sir Robert Baden-Powell (1857–1941), founder of the Scout Movement who, in 1914, put himself at the disposal of the War Office (no command was given to him). Addressing them, he said that 2,000 Scouts were carrying out coastguard duty around the shores, setting men at liberty for service in the navy. He said that many Westmorland Scouts would like to be useful in that way and should remember that, from their training, there were many other ways in which a Scout could be useful.

CHAPTER EIGHT

Keeping the Lakeland Economy Going

Herbert Bell, born in Ambleside in 1856, was a perceptive social commentator, using his camera to record the real face of everyday life in Ambleside. He produced a collection of photographs of ordinary people from washerwomen to sheep-shearers going about their daily tasks, and his archives are in the Armitt Museum, Ambleside. The work, about everyday life, provided a dramatic and telling contrast to the romantic image of Lakeland.

Industry

There was a temporary wartime cessation of slate-quarrying in the Lake District. Unlike the production of khaki, munitions or meat, the industry could not thrive on war. A report on 7 February 1916 said: 'The best hope which the temporary cessation of quarrying in the Lake District affords is that the adaptable men thrown out may soon find remunerative work on the land, in their own neighbourhood.'

Meanwhile, orders began to flood in at Stott Park Bobbin Mill (a working mill from 1835 to 1971) near Newby Bridge for the cotton reels but also for unusual things such as rungs for rope ladders for the Royal Navy, handles and shafts for the tools to dig the hundreds of miles of new trenches on the Western Front, and for the handles for hand grenades. Trench warfare led to the development of new weapons such as the Stokes trench mortar and the modification of others such as the Mills bomb hand grenade. This proved essential as the German army continued to develop numerous models of grenade.

Water-powered gunpowder production in South Lakeland began in 1764 with the Sedgwick Gunpowder Works on the River Kent. Charcoal, a principal ingredient of gunpowder, was a product of the local coppice woods. According to *The Gunpowder Mills of Westmorland and Furness* by Paul N. Wilson (1964), the industry reached its greatest prosperity between around 1860 and the end of the Great War.

Lowwood, near Haverthwaite, and Elterwater, in the Langdale Valley, are two sites that show clear remains of the once-thriving black powder or gunpowder industry. After 1807, Lowwood Gunpowder Works (founded 1798, closed 1934) switched largely to the manufacture of blasting powder and supplied the whole country including the army and navy. The Elterwater Gunpowder Works (opened 1824, closed 1930) supplied local slate quarries with blasting powder.

The following has been taken from *Cumbria Within Living Memory* and relates to memories of the Great War:

> I remember the gunpowder carts on their way to Windermere station each day (from Elterwater), usually twelve, a certain distance apart, in case of accident. The drivers had to walk there, but could ride coming back when the carts were empty. Powder was carted also to many quarries: Kirkby and Low Wood in Furness, Gatebeck and other places below Kendal and Honister. When going to Honister they left Elterwater soon after midnight, when there would be very little other traffic on the roads. On May Day the drivers decorated their horses and the best decorated got a prize. They were paraded around the village, and they always stopped outside the school for the children to come and see them.

In May 1915, a war bonus at the rate of 2s to married men and 1s.6d to single men per week was paid by the Elterwater Gunpowder Works. In view of the great price rises in many of the commodities of life and the small wages paid by the company, the above was looked upon as a substantial increase. The gunpowder works were exceptionally busy and had recently started several fresh hands, both men and women. The *WG* of 23 September 1916 reported that four workmen had been killed in an explosion at the Elterwater Gunpowder Works. The cause was a mystery.

The line from Haverthwaite to Lakeside, which remains open as a heritage railway, passes through a once-thriving Backbarrow, a village that lies on the River Leven where terraced housing was built in the late 1700s to house the industrial workforce of the blast furnaces. Backbarrow Blue Mill is best remembered for the production of the blue pigment ultramarine, or 'dolly blue', that made the whites seem brighter. There was no production from 1913 to 1918. However, this was due to a fire in the ancillary shed in 1913 that spread to the whole of the south mill. During the factory's operation (it closed in 1981), the whole area around it had a blue tinge and, in later years, workers from Ulverston had their own special bus service because they were so covered in blue. Private William Bellman (1879–1955) of Chapel House, Backbarrow, formerly a boiler fireman employed at the Ultramarine Works, was

Lowwood Gunpowder Works, Clock Tower and buildings in 1981, now the Clock Tower Business Centre. (*Courtesy of Kevin Statham*)

Lowwood gunpowder van, c.1930. Horses shod with copper or brass shoes were used to pull the 'trams' along rails across the river bridge and then up the steep gradient to Haverthwaite station. (*Courtesy of Kevin Statham*)

Backbarrow Blue Mill (undated). Today, the Lakeland Motor Museum is located on the site of the former mill. (*southlakes-uk*)

conscripted, as reported by the *Barrow News* of 2 June 1917. After the war, Windermere gardener Fred Wills (1895–1963), Border Regiment, worked at the Backbarrow Blue Mill for many years. He joined the army at the start of the Great War and did garrison duty for five years, mostly at Maymyo, Burma.

In 1911, a French concern was established, called the Coniston Electrolytic Copper Company, to reprocess the huge spoil heaps close to old mine buildings. Henri de Varinay was in charge and arrived in September. He was a larger-than-life character and proved to be a hit with the villagers. By April 1914, all the required machinery had been assembled and three Frenchmen and eighteen local workers were ready to make copper out of piles of rubbish. It had the makings of being a success but the Great War got in the way and the French experts were recalled. In 1915, it was under British control but closed soon after.

Footwear for the army

Kendal shoemaker K Shoes was founded in 1842 by Robert Miller Somervell. By 1913, production had reached a total of 230,526 pairs. However, the outbreak of war saw the factory emptied of all able-bodied men of fighting age and the women and older men were left working on

'K Marching Boots', leather leggings, 'K Service Boots for Officers' and major contracts for the French and Russian armies. The year 1917 saw what has been described by the National Union of Boot and Shoe Operatives as a 'trail-blazing agreement' with the workers: a 49.5-hour week, a week's paid holiday a year and time and a half for all overtime. After the Second World War, factories were opened in Workington (closed 1980), Millom (closed 2006), Askam-in-Furness (closed 1997) and Shap (closed 1999). K Shoes' factory in Kendal closed in 2003. Twenty-two men are named on the K Shoes War Memorial and all have addresses in Kendal.

Agriculture

On 13 February 1915, it was reported in the *WG* that the farmers and milk-sellers of Ambleside had decided, owing to the increased price of feeding stuff, to raise the price of milk from 3d to 4d per quart. A protest had been issued against this, concluding that the 'good folk of Ambleside will not be exploited'.

The editorial in the *Carlisle Journal* on 9 March 1915 said:

Everyone must admit the need of maintaining the activity of the agricultural industry in time of war, when the question of food supply is of supreme importance, and that any shortage of labour which hinders or curtails the operations of the farm must, if possible, be made good. Even the employment of boy labour ought not be prohibited if no other means of carrying on the work of the farm can be devised.

There was a large advert in the local press on 16 June 1915 addressed 'To the Farmers of Cumberland and Westmorland': 'The Army Council has decided that in view of the shortage of agricultural labour for the hay harvest, furlough will be given to a limited number of Soldiers of the New Armies and of the Territorial Force for work in the hay harvest as circumstances may permit.' (Furlough is a period of time that a worker or a soldier is allowed to be absent, especially to return temporarily to their own town or country.)

By 1917, food production had become a matter of grave national importance as U-boats targeted British merchant vessels and rationing was introduced. Marian Atkinson, aged 97 in 2003, spoke to oral historians Richard van Emden and Steve Humphries. She grew up in the Lake District and was a 12-year-old schoolgirl in 1917:

We'd see turnips, potatoes and cabbage and we'd decide what we'd pinch on the way home. On the way back, the bigger boys used to

say 'Keep your eyes rolling for the farmer'. My parents wouldn't
accept anything stolen – they used to make us take it back – so we
used to sit under a hedge and gnaw the vegetables like a rabbit. If we
could hear the farmers' horses clip-clopping, we used to bung what
we'd been eating under the hedge and go like lightning back home,
large as life.

The *WG* reported on 27 January 1917 that the War Agricultural Committee had completed its inspection of farms and private land in Grasmere that was considered suitable for ploughing and made the following
recommendations:

1. That the owner of the garden in Easedale has land harrowed in
   spring and planted with potatoes.
2. Owner of Above Beck to plant 1 additional acre.
3. Three acres to be ploughed at The Wray.
4. The Close, owner to plough 3 acres.
5. Butterlyp How, tenant to plough 2½ acres.
6. Far Easedale, owner willing to plough 1 acre.

A farmer, one of the ploughing farmers, is willing to assist with any
necessary ploughing. Result of inspection showed about 309 acres
of meadow land, 23 acres ploughed last year, 40 additional acres
offered for ploughing this year and 59 additional acres recom-
mended for ploughing.

'The food controller has made an order prohibiting the making of
crumpets, muffins, tea cakes, fancy breads and pastries. Tea shops are to
be rationed in the supply of sugar and wheaten flour,' the *WG* reported
on 22 April 1917.

On 7 July 1917 the *WG* reported that Mrs Fleming's clippings at
Knott Houses, Grasmere on Monday was in more than one respect a
record. The grand weather allowed the sheep to be easily gathered in and
quickly disposed of. Work began at 8.00am and by 4.30pm more than
900 animals had been relieved of their fleecy covering. Fifty-one workers
sat down to supper and the evening was spent in merriment and song,
after the tradition of many generations of the Flemings at Knott Houses.

A list of foods for which maximum retail prices applied was printed in
the *WG* on 8 September 1917: wheat and all cereals, beef, veal, mutton,
lamb, pork, butter, bacon, ham, lard, sugar, cheap tea, cheap coffee,
sweets, jams, juices, dried beans, dried peas, herrings, oats, oatmeal,
maize foods.

In January 1918, there was a meeting of the Grasmere Food Control
Committee. A priority scheme was needed for children in the event of

a milk shortage (*Whitehaven News*, 24 January 1918). At a meeting of Grasmere Urban District Council, the *WG* reported on 8 June 1918, it was suggested that the hauling wagons taking timber out of Grasmere daily could return with articles for general use like food and coal. The council agreed to provide a supply of coal for the poor people of the village who bought coal by the bag. The traction engines could easily bring in 20 tons per week. It was agreed that a weighing machine needed to be purchased and the question of transport to be followed up by members of the committee appointed by the Central Food Committee.

Visitors during the war
Although the influx of tourists and 'off-comers' began in earnest in the early nineteenth century, the coming of the railway to Windermere in 1847 (the Kendal and Windermere Railway with stops at Staveley and Burneside) and the launching of the lake's first passenger steamer service in 1845, *Lady of the Lake* (she continued in service until 1865), opened the floodgates to a major expansion and redevelopment of the town.

In the early years of the twentieth century, charabancs – early motor coaches, usually open-topped and perilous – were used from Windermere

Vroom with a view: a public charabanc at Kirkstone Pass, which connects Ambleside in the Rothay Valley to Patterdale in the Ullswater Valley, c.1900.

station to provide a number of circular tours. The *WG* on 10 April 1915 reported that Easter brought more visitors than was anticipated. The hotels and private hotels in Grasmere were full, and some of the lodging houses had parties but more of them were empty. 'The greatest contrast to other Easters was to be met with on the roads – a few pedestrians and a few motor cars, where in other years there were streams.' The *WG* reported on 29 May 1915 that, while the season was a good one, the complete absence of American tourists and the withdrawal of cheap bookings had had an adverse effect on places such as Dove Cottage. However, the hotels were full to overflowing and a party of Scouts who had come into Easedale from Manchester Grammar were having a good time, the weather being ideal for camping.

There was a serious charabanc accident near Belsfield, Windermere on Friday, 9 July 1915 when the vehicle struck a stone culvert. The side was ripped off the vehicle and one passenger, a woman, died two days later. The charabanc was running an excursion – a 'sharra trip' – from Blackpool to Windermere.

On 21 July 1915, local newspapers carried a letter from Canon Rawnsley:

> It has come to my knowledge that some who were intending to come to the Lake District for their holiday have been put off by hearing that in consequence of the war, the holiday makers who would otherwise have gone to the Continent or to the East Coast have thronged the district, and that accommodation is not to be had. I wish to give an emphatic contradiction to the rumour. The scarcity of visitors is felt throughout the Lake Country.

In August 1915, Mary Augusta Ward wrote that generally the tiny house and garden of Dove Cottage were thronged by Americans in August

> who crowd – in the Homeric phrase – about the charming place, like flies about the milk pails in summer. But this year there are no Americans, there are few visitors, indeed, of any kind as yet, though the coaches are beginning to bring them, scantily. But Grasmere does not distress itself as it would in other years, Wordsworth's village is thinking too much about the war.

According to the *WG* on 14 April 1917, the number of visitors in Grasmere was smaller than ever remembered. The hotels were fairly well filled but as the Prince of Wales Hotel, Grasmere was closed the shortage was more real than apparent. The church services were well-attended. Bank Holiday was as quiet as any ordinary week.

Discover Wordsworth (1779–1850): Dove Cottage, Grasmere, the poet's first family home where mighty poets gathered and poetry that England will never let die was written. (*Wikipedia*)

According to the *WG* on 6 April 1918, Grasmere was very busy, the number of visitors being larger than for the past two or three years. The hotels were full, with sleepers out, and all the larger residential houses were occupied. There were the usual church services on Easter Day. The *WG* reported on 25 April 1918 that Grasmere was full, with more visitors since the war had begun.

CHAPTER NINE

Keeping Up Traditions

Grasmere Sports

The annual Grasmere Sports has been a regular event since 1868, unbroken except for the periods of the two world wars. Participants can compete in a number of sports including Cumberland Wrestling, a good-natured form of physical combat. Henry Walsh was a champion Cumberland wrestler, winning between 1910 and 1912. He was brought up in Frizington, west Cumbria and was one of many First World War soldiers gassed in battle. Sent back to the UK to recuperate, he died soon after, aged just 27.

Revived on Wednesday, 20 August 1919, the Grasmere Sports saw a post-war wrestling boom, according to the *Yorkshire Post and Leeds Intelligencer* on 22 August 1919, after a lapse of six years:

> A gloomy morning preceded a beautiful day, and all roads that led to the beautiful vale, grand stand, and ring, were crowded with dense masses of people, including many society folk. Lord Lonsdale and party were present, and among others present were Major-General A.A. Kennedy, Mr. de Courcey Parry, Mr. A.B. Dunlop and party, Colonel and Mrs. Kennedy, Mr. R.H. Curry, Lieut.-Colonel Fothergill, Mr. P.J. Hibbert, Commander S.W.B. Kennedy, and Colonel Haworth (High Sheriff). The sports themselves were quite equal to their high reputation, and entries in wrestling were considerably in advance of pre-war sports. In addition to light-weight, middle-weight, and heavy-weight wrestling, there was also a guides' race to the top of Castle Rock, a climb in view of the ground, which was accomplished in just over 14 minutes; and a hound trail of 9 miles, passing over the foot of Helvellyn and Fairfield. Pole leaping and jumping, and flat races were also held. Some of the best runners in the country being held.

The 1919 champions were as follows:

Heavyweight wrestling: R. Graham
Middleweight wrestling: J.S. Robinson

(*Left*) Champion Cumberland wrestler Henry Walsh. (*Courtesy of the Walsh family*)

(*Right*) Lance Corporal Ernest Harford Dalzell, 1st Borders, died on 19 May 1917. He was a famous Cumberland and Westmorland fell runner who was a star of the Grasmere Sports. He is remembered on the Keswick War Memorial. (*Courtesy of the Dalzell family*)

> Lightweight wrestling: A. Holliday
> Guides' Race: J. Pooley
> Pole leap: M.H. Dickinson
> High leap: C.E. Bergmeler
> Long jump: C.E. Bergmeler

The Great War took its toll on Ambleside Sports, which includes Cumberland Wrestling. In 1920, Ambleside Sports were resumed and held on Miller Field but they soon lapsed until after the Second World War. The Grizedale Hall Hound Trail was cancelled in September 1914 in consequence of the war.

Grasmere Rushbearing

Rushbearing is a festival associated with the ancient custom of annually replacing the rushes on the earth floors of churches, rushes being a general term for rushes, reeds and sweet-smelling grasses. St Oswald's church floor was paved in 1840 and it was no longer necessary to strew rushes; the ceremony, however, continues. Grasmere Rushbearing – which in 2015 was on 20 July and is now principally a children's festival – starts at the village school in Stock Lane and winds its way to the village green where there is a short service and singing. Many of the bearings are traditional emblems that appear year after year. One just says 'Peace' and was introduced after the First World War.

In Grasmere Village Hall, there is a painting of the Rushbearing by artist Frank Bramley (1857–1915), who by 1900 had settled with his

The Grasmere Rushbearing by Frank Bramley, RA (1857–1915). The oil on canvas is in the care of National Trust Collections. (*The National Trust*)

wife Katherine Graham at Belle Vue Cottage (now Orchard Cottage), Easedale Road, Grasmere. In 1911, they lived at gentleman's residence Tongue Ghyll, Grasmere, where they had two servants, Elizabeth Thompson and Annie Green. The painting was exhibited at the Royal Academy, London in 1913. Grasmere Rushbearing was held as usual in July 1915 but without the accompanying gala. There was 'ideal weather and a bright show' for Grasmere Rushbearing in July/August 1916, but there was no band to accompany the procession that year. In 1917, the weather was all that could be wished for. There was an abundance of flowers and the village was full of visitors. The *WG* of 11 August 1917 reported:

> Gingerbread was given out, this has happened without a break for 80 years. The six maidens were: Connie Smith, Alice Proctor, Nellie Davidson, Jean Sanderson, Annie Lomas, Mary Whitam. There was no band but the children sang the Rushbearing Hymn. After making a round of the village the bearings were taken into the church and a service was sung by the rector.

Victorian cook Sarah Nelson invented Grasmere Gingerbread in the village in 1854. Today, the Grasmere Gingerbread Shop is run by third-generation owners Joanne and Andrew Hunter.

CHAPTER TEN

Beatrix Potter:
The Land and the War

Children's author Helen Beatrix Potter (1866–1943) was a Unitarian from Manchester. Unitarian Universalists object to war in their sixth principle: 'The goal of world community with peace, liberty and justice for all.'

Potter, who was born in Bolton Gardens, Chelsea – where her parents, who had inherited wealth from cotton manufacturing, employed a number of servants – had spent many holidays in the Lake District. She watched Lord Lonsdale's party at the Keswick Country House Hotel with the Kaiser on 14 August 1895, and recorded the following entry in her diary about the procession:

> August 15 1895. We consumed three whole hours waiting to see the Emperor, not very well worth it. I had seen him in London. I think he is stouter. I was not particularly excited. I think it is disgraceful to drive fine horses like that. First came a messenger riding a good roan belonging to Bowness, which we could hear snorting before they came in sight, man and horse both dead-beat. He reported the Emperor would be up in ten minutes, but it was twenty.
>
> The procession consisted of a mounted policeman with a drawn sword in a state approaching apoplexy, the red coats of the Quorn Hunt, four or five of Lord Lonsdale's carriages, several hires and spare horses straggling after them. There were two horses with an outside rider to each carriage, splendid chestnut thoroughbreds floundering along and clinking their shoes.
>
> They were not going fast when we saw them, having come all the way from Patterdale without even stopping at Kirkstone to water the horses, to the indignation of mine host, and an assembly of three or four hundred who had reckoned on this act of mercy. I think his majesty deserved an accident and rather wonder he didn't have one

considering the smallness of the little Tiger sitting on the box to work the break [*sic*].

The liveries were blue and yellow and the carriages much yellow singularly ugly low tub. With a leather top to shut up sideways. [NB: This is in original diary note form, hence the unconventional style.] The Emperor, Lord Lonsdale and two ladies in the first, Lady Dudley etc in the second.

There was a considerable crowd and very small flags. German ones hard to get at short notice, but plenty of tricolours. Lord Lonsdale is red-headed and has a harum-scarum reputation, but according to Mr Edmondson, less 'stupid' than his predecessor whom he had seen 'Beastly droonk' in the road on a Sunday morning.

In 1905, Beatrix decided to use some of the income from her books and a legacy from her aunt to buy a seventeenth-century Lakeland farm in Sawrey called Hill Top. She arranged for an extension to be built on the house so that the farm manager, John Cannon, could continue to live there with his family and run the farm, with its pigs, cows, sheep, ducks and hens. Although Potter was still living at home in London, she spent as much time as she could in visiting her new home.

In 1910, she employed her skills as writer and illustrator to campaign against free trade with Germany (local toy manufacturers struggling against the tide of German Peter Rabbit soft toys), and the Liberal government's census of horses. It came at a time of rising tensions between Britain and Germany. The government had assured the owners that the census was not for taxation purposes or for use by the military authorities, but it was in reality for the conscription of horses in a great national emergency. She campaigned against working farm horses being conscripted if conflict broke out. 'No doubt we should be paid for our horses,' she wrote in a leaflet titled *The Shortage of Horses*, 'but what about our ruined crops?'

She married William Heelis (1892–1945), a local solicitor from Hawkshead, in 1913. Some of his nephews left in August 1914 for the war and Beatrix had news that her brother Bertram (1872–1918) had volunteered but, somewhat to her relief, had been refused on account of his frail health. In June 1918, Bertram died of a brain haemorrhage.

On 18 May 1915, in a letter to her editor Harold Warne, she said: 'I do hope your nephews are all alive and unhurt – or not badly. Sometimes it is a relief to have them safe in hospital.' Her nephew Second Lieutenant Hilary Loraine Heelis (1898–1938) joined the army on 1 June 1916 as a private soldier, giving his prior occupation as 'school lad'. He became an officer with the Lancashire Fusiliers in 1917 and was taken prisoner of war (PoW) in France on 4 June 1918 during a trench raid. He returned to Britain, married Winifred Tootill (1901–73) in 1926 and died, aged 40, at Bridge House, Bradshaw, Bolton, Lancashire.

According to author Margaret Speaker-Yuan, in her book *Beatrix Potter* (Kyle Zimmer, 2005), Potter lost a distant set of cousins when the *Lusitania* was torpedoed. From *Beatrix Potter* by Judy Taylor, it appears that one of those cousins was Bobbie Pearce.

Potter had firm opinions about women's ability to do farm work, thinking that they could have a better life in the fresh air than toiling in the munitions factories. She wrote a letter on the subject that was published in *The Times* (10 March 1916) under the pseudonym 'A Woman Farmer':

> Sir,
>
> In your leader upon the employment of women you say that the chief step is the offer of adequate wages. The custom of employing women upon farms has never quite ceased in the north, but the supply of women is undoubtedly affected by the competition of munition work. I pass no opinion as to whether munition workers are extravagantly paid; I only know that farmers cannot compete with their wages. Three girls have gone from adjoining farms here; they expect to earn at least £2 wages per week. They are trained dairymaids and milkers, but totally inexperienced in mechanics. The present waste of skilled training is unfortunate. At one and the same time I was receiving from a Labour Exchange advice to take outside women on my farm; from another Labour Exchange requests for the character of my cowman's daughters for munitions; and my little general servant was being canvassed to go on the land (from which I should presumably have been removed to do the housework). I have worked on it for years and love it; but I still feel some sympathy with the perplexity of the farmers. Harm is being done by the ridiculous and vulgar photographs which appear in the Press. I am perfectly ready to employ the right sort of woman. French women and North country girls have found it possible to work in a short petticoat, and they have not required the theatrical attractions of uniform and armlet to induce them to do their duty.
>
> Yours truly,
A Woman Farmer

As a result of this letter, Eleanor Louisa (Louie) Choyce (1876–1963) – who had been the governess to a wealthy family in Gloucestershire – went to work for her. Hill Top now boasted a sizeable flock of chickens,

Beatrix Potter and Canon Rawnsley, who encouraged her to publish her first book
The Tale of Peter Rabbit. (*The National Trust*)

turkeys and some ducks which produced income but also provided food on the farm. Rationing and wartime shortages meant that even rabbits were raised as farm stock. Potter, best remembered for her books such as *The Tale of Peter Rabbit*, confessed she did not like having them killed. She continued to allow the Guides the use of her land for camping throughout the war.

Potter died at Castle Cottage, Near Sawrey, after suffering a cold from which she could not recover, aged 77. She was cremated and her ashes scattered by her husband on the spot in Near Sawrey where they had often walked. In her will, much of her property was bequeathed to the National Trust.

A million horses were sent to France to fight in the Great War and only 62,000 came back. Horses pulled guns, ration carts and ambulances by day and night, often in terrible conditions. An advert on page one of the *Daily Telegraph* of 13 February 1915 by the Purple Cross Service called for donations to relieve the suffering of war horses. Michael Morpurgo's novel *War Horse* (1982) and the play and film based upon it have in recent years thrown a spotlight on the equine contribution to the Great War.

Also the intelligent work of homing pigeons often meant the difference between life and death in the delivery of important communications. Pigeons were used to send rescue messages back and forth from soldiers to their base. Potter wrote *The Tale of the Faithful Dove* in 1908 about a pigeon called Mr Vidler (published posthumously).

CHAPTER ELEVEN

Stories of Local War Heroes

James William Baisbrown (1880–1964) of Tanner Croft, Grasmere enlisted in Ambleside for the 'duration of the war' on 25 November 1915. After an initial period, he was posted to Windsor on 21 October 1916 and transferred as a private in the Household Brigade, Irish Guards APC (Army Pay Corps). Born in Grasmere, 'Jimmy' was Westmorland's only representative in the Household Brigade (which was formed to reinforce the Household Cavalry so severely depleted during the Battle of the Somme). He saw service in France with the British Expeditionary Force (BEF) between 3 February 1917 and 28 April 1918. He returned to Tanner Croft, Grasmere to his pre-war job of grocer's assistant at J.J. Foster, Red Lion Square, bringing up his two girls, taking an active part in the British Legion, being closely connected with St Oswald's and village life. He and his wife Annie received a telegram from Her Majesty Queen Elizabeth II on the occasion of their diamond wedding anniversary (4 November 1963). He passed away in January 1964, aged 84.

The *WG* of 1 May 1915 features a photograph of an Ambleside soldier family. Abraham Bowe, a saddler and harness maker, and Jane Bowe, who in 1911 lived in Bridge Street, had five sons serving their country in a military capacity. Leonard Bowe (1873–1943), a mason's labourer, and Abraham Bowe (1881–1964), a stone mason, were in Egypt; John Bowe (1880–1957), Army Transport Corps (Horse Transport), of Kelsick Cottage was on transport duty in France. Thomas William Bowe (1884–1937) was on guard duty at Grayrigg railway station (closed in 1954), on the course of the original Lancaster and Carlisle Railway between Lancaster and Penrith, and Christopher Bowe (1875–1951), a carter general to corn millers, was helping to guard Arnside railway viaduct on the Furness Line. A grandson, Charles Hemms, was also on transport duty in France. The viaduct, built in 1857, was rebuilt in 1915 to support the extra weight of the munition trains from Barrow. Additional brickwork was added to the piers around the lattice steelwork of the original build.

William Edward Bradley (1898–1918), Army Ordnance Corps, was the son of Thomas Seatle Bradley and Ruth Smith Bradley of Main Street, Hawkshead. He had been to Ballincolig, Ireland on initial training and was returning home on leave on the *Leinster*, bound for Holyhead, when it was torpedoed and sunk by a U-boat on 10 October 1918 just outside Dublin Bay. Bradley was one of the many casualties. The official death toll was 501. The ship's log states that she carried 77 crew and 694 passengers on her final voyage. Also aboard were nurses from Britain, Ireland, Australia, New Zealand, Canada and the United States. The survivors were rescued by HMS *Lively*, HMS *Mallard* and HMS *Seal*. Bradley was buried at Grangegorman Military Cemetery, Dublin. He is remembered on the war memorial at Hawkshead Church and on the Hawkshead Cross.

Gunner Robert Henry Bunting (1884–1970), son of Robert and Margaret Bunting (née Hudson) and born at Town End, Grasmere, served in the Border Regiment in India for four years during the Great War and was awarded the British War Medal and Victory Medal. His first job was working part-time as an errand boy for an Ambleside confectioner-cum-corn-and-straw merchant, where he drove his first vehicle, a small pony and float. At 14, he tried his hand at painting for two years, all the time cycling from Grasmere to Ambleside on a solid-tyred bicycle. He then drove coaches from the Salutation Hotel in Ambleside and in winter he used to cart slates from Elterwater to Windermere station and, on his return, supplies for the Co-op stores. In 1920, he joined the Lake District Road Traffic, proprietors of chara-bancs. He later drove 'Bob's bus', the Ferry-Ambleside route, from 1945 to the end of 1954. He became more than a just a driver; he became guardian of schoolchildren and an errand-runner. When he retired, he was immediately missed by dozens of regular users. Bunting married Elsie McCabe (b.1894) in 1913 and they had one child.

Major Aubone Charles Campbell (1888–1918), King's Own Scottish Borderers, son of Mr and Mrs Robert Campbell of Silver Howe, served seven years in his regiment before the start of the Great War. Campbell, who was born in France, had returned home on 26 September 1915, leaving Boulogne for Dover on SS *Dieppe* with shrapnel wounds. In a letter to the War Office on 2 March 1916, held at TNA, he wrote:

> I have the honour to submit this my application for a wound gratuity. I was hit on September 24th 1915 by a shrapnel ball, in the back of the head, which narrowly missed the spine and artery.

Bob Bunting with the Eight Lakes Tour bus.

I have, since receiving this wound, suffered very considerably from neuralgia which, at present, periodically incapacitates me from work. In addition I now suffer from insomnia. Trusting this application will receive your favourable consideration.

He was reported fit for war service on 19 February 1916 by the War Office and therefore ordered to join the battalion. He was recorded as wounded (multiple) on 26 March 1918 while serving with the BEF during the German Operation MICHAEL and died at the 3rd Canadian Station Hospital at Doullens, France on 3 April 1918.

His DSO citation read as follows in the *London Gazette* of 26 July 1918:

Maj. Aubone Charles Campbell, R. Scots. (Capt., K.O.S.B.). For conspicuous gallantry and devotion to duty, when for six days he handled his battalion in a series of rearguard actions, and was seriously wounded. At a critical moment he personally commanded the battalion rearguard, and once succeeded in slipping away when the enemy was right round his flank.

His grave, at Doullens Communal Cemetery, was marked by a durable wooden cross with an inscription bearing full particulars. He is remembered at St Oswald's.

Walter Dent and Thomas William Dent were sons of James and Elizabeth Dent of Station Road, Keswick. Lance Corporal Walter Dent (1882–1915), Border, originally enlisted in 1901 at Carlisle Castle. He later went on the reserve and was recalled to the colours in August 1914 at which time he was a postman at Windermere. The battalion landed in Zeebrugge on 6 October 1914. They moved down to billets in Sailly sur la Lys, and were entrenched near Cordonnerie Farm where he was killed on 23 January 1915. He left a wife and six children under the age of 9 at Stanley Terrace, Birch Street, Windermere. He is remembered in the first column on the Windermere Cenotaph memorial.

Thomas 'Tommy' William Dent (1877–1917) also fell. He enlisted at Colne, Lancashire, in October 1916. He went into the trenches for the first time on 14 February 1917 at Sailly sur la Lys. On 11 March, he was reported Missing – believed prisoner. This detail is later struck through on his casualty record. He was buried at Pont-du-Hem Military Cemetery, La Gourge, west of Sailly. Tommy left a wife Mary and five children. W. Dent and T.W. Dent are commemorated on the front of Keswick War Memorial. Both Walter Dent and Thomas William Dent are on the Keswick Roll of Honour.

The RAMC was not a fighting force but its members saw the full horror of war. Lieutenant Reginald Hannay Fothergill (1879–1971), son of George and Ada Joan Fothergill of Allan Bank, Grasmere, attended Old College preparatory school in Windermere and then Repton College. He qualified as a doctor at Edinburgh University and lived and worked at Dalton-in-Furness prior to the outbreak of war. The *London Gazette* of February 1915 states that on 21 January 1915 Reginald Hannay Fothergill, MB of the Army Medical Corps was made temporary lieutenant. On 21 January 1916, he was made temporary captain. He was wounded in 1916 and returned to Dalton after the war.

On 6 February 1915, the *WG* reported the sorrow expressed in Ambleside on learning of the death of Second Lieutenant Francis Henry Stanley Hawkesworth (1895–1915), 3rd Border, second son of the vicar of Ambleside, Reverend John Hawkesworth (1867–1922). Reverend Hawkesworth and his wife Frances (b.1868, née Ledlie) – both born in Ireland – raised seven sons. On 12 February 1915, a letter from Reverend Hawkesworth of The Vicarage, originally published in the parish magazine, was reprinted in the *Lakes Herald*. In the letter, he thanked those who had sent him messages of support and sympathy after the death of his son who was killed in action in Givenchy, France on 25 January 1915. The vicar wrote:

> God knows in all humility that if such a sorrow was to come to any home in the parish it should come first to the Vicarage, where it ought to be borne with courage and resignation. If it were God's will that any young men were to lay down their lives for their country, Stanley would be proud and glad to be the first.

Frances Hawkesworth, Stanley's mother, who lived and worked at the Lyndhurst house in Newby Bridge in the late 1920s and early 1930s. (Westmorland Gazette)

Hawkesworth, who was going to become a missionary, was the fifth ex-St Bees pupil to be killed in action. William Leefe Robinson (1895–1918), who was awarded the Victoria Cross (VC) for shooting down a German airship over Britain on 2/3 September 1916, said: 'The war is sickening, the other day I heard of the death of a great friend of mine at school, Hawkesworth by name – we all called him "Nailer" – he was one of the best of fellows.' He is on the Le Touret memorial and the St Bees school ROH.

Frank Herbert (b.1890), who had a shop in Windermere, joined the army when war broke out. His brother Louis Herbert (1882–1970), who ran the photographic business with his brother, had his sights on the Royal Navy, possibly because he had been enthralled by the planes that flew from Lake Windermere.

Herbert's for Kodaks: Frank Herbert posing outside his shop in Windermere, opposite St Martin's Church. (*Courtesy of the Lakes Flying Company*)

In the RNAS, which Louis Herbert joined on 16 January 1917, he continued to work as a photographer (one of his photos is taken from an airship showing a British seaplane in flight). His first posting was to the training establishment at Crystal Palace and then in March 1917 he went to headquarters at Chingford before being posted two months later to the dreadnought battleship HMS *Queen Elizabeth*, then serving in the Atlantic. He spent nine months with No. 6 Wing RNAS, much of it at the small Italian town of Trento, which was well inland. He was transferred in April 1918 to the RAF and in August 1918 was posted to the airship station at Howden, Yorkshire, followed by a move to Heaton Park, Manchester, where he seems to have stayed until he was demobbed into the RAF Reserve in February 1919. His service papers show him 'deemed discharged' on 30 April 1920. Despite his age, he volunteered for four years in the reserve at Cardington as an AC2 Photographer on 12 May 1939 and on his officer's recommendation he was promoted to leading aircraftsman the next day. After the war he continued running the photographic business with his brother Frank. Louis died in 1970 and was buried at Windermere in a grave next to that of his son Jack, who had died as a teenager in a climbing accident.

Coniston's best-known First World War soldier was Lance Corporal James Hewitson (1892–1963), 1/4th Battalion KO, whose parents

James Hewitson receives his VC from King George V.

farmed at Waterhead Farm, Torver. He was awarded the VC in 1918. On 26 April 1918, at Givenchy, France, in a daylight attack on a series of crater posts, Lance Corporal Hewitson led his party to their objective, clearing the enemy from both trench and dugouts, killing six who would not surrender. After capturing the final objective, he saw a hostile machine-gun team coming into action against his men. Working his way round the edge of the crater, he attacked the team, killing four and capturing one. Shortly afterwards he routed a bombing party that was attacking a Lewis gun, killing six of them. He died on 2 March 1963 in Ulverston and is buried in St Andrew's churchyard, Coniston. His medal is privately held.

The Coniston Church of England School First World War ROH, previously at the school in Shepherd's Bridge Lane, Coniston, has been lost. Twenty-nine men were named, including Hewitson. Twenty-two served and returned; seven died.

Major Hero Wilhelm Oswald Hillerns (1882–1917) was killed in action on 14 April 1917. An architect by profession, he had trained in both New York and Paris. He had visited his family in Grasmere just a few days prior to his death, after serving for eighteen months at the front with the Royal Field Artillery. According to the accounts of eyewitnesses, he was killed in action near Arras by a shell while out reconnoitring for a new gun position. Together with three other officers, he had gone forward towards the front line to find a new gun position for the battery when they were caught by sudden shelling. The other two officers escaped with wounds, but Hillerns and another officer were hit in the head by fragments of a shell and died instantly. He was killed at the start of the Battle of Arras, during the First Battle of the Scarpe, which was a strong allied success, allowing them to take control of the strategic German trenches between Wancourt and Feuchy. He was Mentioned in Despatches by Sir Douglas Haig (*London Gazette*, 18 May 1917) for gallant and distinguished service in the field. He is buried at Beaurains

The missing Roll of Honour. (Westmorland Gazette)

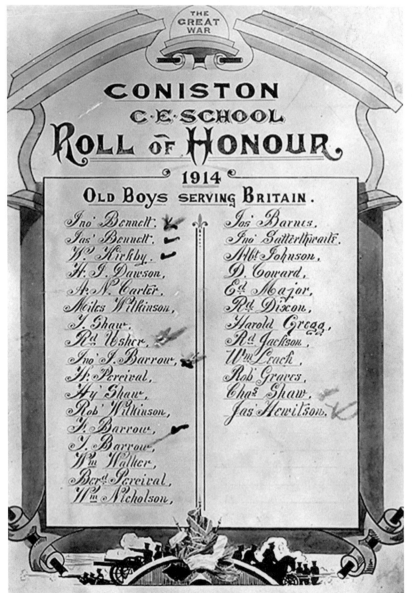

Post Office telegram (held at Kew archives) informing parents that Caleb Walden Margerison was wounded. (*Author*)

Road Cemetery, Beaurains, northern France, and remembered on the slate war memorial inside St Oswald's.

Lance Sergeant Ernest McKnight (d.1916), 11th Border, lived in Belfast and enlisted in Windermere. Badly wounded on 1 July 1916, he tended the wounds of his officer Lieutenant Caleb Walden Margerison (1895–1916), 11th Border, then crawled back into Authuille Wood, Somme to die. McKnight lies in the Lonsdale Cemetery. Margerison, an old Reptonian who was educated at Trinity College, Cambridge and whose parents lived at the Wynlass Beck Victorian mansion, Windermere, was wounded on 1 July 1916 and died of his wounds in hospital in France on 6 July 1916. He is buried at Warloy-Baillon Communal Cemetery Extension, Picardy, France. McKnight and Margerison are both on the Windermere St Mary memorial and Windermere Cenotaph. The Repton School War Memorial contains 355 names. Margerison is among the names for school leavers 1908–1915 who lost their lives in the Great War.

On the morning of 10 May 1918, it was ascertained that a Zeppelin was working off Heligoland, a small German archipelago in the North Sea that under the German Empire became a major naval base. Soon after 1.00pm, a Felixstowe F2A flying boat (F2A N4291) – with Captain Thomas Cooper Pattinson (1890–1971), an architect from Elme Bank, Windermere, and Captain Albert Henry Munday (1890–1957), an Eton-educated Australian-born Canadian, as pilots – left Killingholme, North Lincolnshire to hunt her down.

The Felixstowe F2 was developed by Lieutenant
Commander John Cyril Porte (1884–1919), who
before the war had worked with American
aircraft designer Glenn Curtiss (1878–1930) on a
flying boat, the America. (*Wikipedia*)

Thomas Cooper Pattinson, 1936.
(*Courtesy of his family*)

After a three-and-a-half-hour flight, the Zeppelin (LZ 107) was sighted a mile away heading for Heligoland. The boat's crew immediately stood by the machine guns, while Pattinson climbed to 6,000ft and overtook the airship. The Zeppelin had, however, seen the boat. Increasing her height, the airship endeavoured to get directly above to drop bombs on her aggressor. Rapid fire was opened by the boat at 500 yards' range, and although all the bullets appeared to hit, the airship continued to climb and, when directly over the boat, dropped five or six bombs that fell harmlessly into the sea.

The race for height continued and when the boat reached 11,000ft, fire was opened on the target some 1,500ft higher up. The boat was now 60 miles off Heligoland and, as the port engine began to give trouble, the pilot was compelled to turn for home.

The Zeppelin went down in flames. However, the closing act of the drama was not witnessed by those who had brought about her destruction as they were busy looking to their own safety, according to *German Air Raids on Britain 1914–1918* by Joseph Morris. The flying boat had been compelled to land at sea on account of a faulty oil pipe. On perceiving this, German destroyers that had fired at the boat during her encounter with the Zeppelin at once made for the apparently ship-

Heligoland islands. During the Great War, the civilian population was evacuated to the mainland. (*Wikipedia*)

wrecked aviators but they were frustrated. Despite a very heavy sea, Sergeant Henry Robert Stubbington (1893–1976) from Portsmouth, the engineer, climbed on top of the offending engine, repaired the oil pipe, and within fifteen minutes the boat was in the air on a safe homeward journey. The fourth man in the Felixstowe was Air Mechanic Johnson.

Pattinson was awarded the DFC (Distinguished Flying Cross). He married Gladys Mary Ives in 1917 in Guiseley, Yorkshire, and his son George Harry was born on 3 August 1918. He was one of the earliest members of the Rotary Club of Windermere, and was captain of the Windermere Home Guard.

Pattinson died at Rayrigg Hall. Pattinson's son George was a local builder and boat collector. He opened the Windermere Steamboat Museum in 1977. In its heyday, it attracted 80,000 visitors each year but closed in 2006. The museum is due to re-open in 2017 as the Windermere Jetty Museum of Boats, Steam and Stories.

Second Lieutenant William Carter Preston (1894–1918), 8th Border, son of Thomas and Sara Ann Preston, lived at Fold Farm, Far Sawrey, between Hawkshead and Lake Windermere. He studied and worked as an architect before the First World War. The 8th Border was in line between the rivers Douvre and Lys on 9 April 1918 (French-Belgian Flanders). While Preston was instructing a unit of men on 10 April 1918, he was shot by a sniper and he died among friends on his position at Laclytte, Reninghurst. He was liked by his comrades who gave him the nickname WC (William Carter). He has no known grave. He was commemorated with honour on the Ploegsteert Memorial, is named on the Ambleside Memorial in St Mary's churchyard, and on a plaque in the chancel at St Peter's Church, Far Sawrey.

Sergeant Thomas Henry Sanderson (1891–1917), RFA, the eldest son of Thomas Mounsey Sanderson of Red Lion Cottage, died of chest wounds on 17 August 1917 while in action during the Battle of Passchendaele and is buried at Brandhoek New Military Cemetery, Belgium. He is remembered at St Oswald's. He won the DCM in April 1916 and his success gave great satisfaction to all his friends in Grasmere (*WG*, 15 April 1916). He had been in Grasmere just three months prior to his death when he married Miss Nellie Postlethwaite. A public meeting was held on Saturday, 2 June 1917 to present him with a gold watch subscribed for by the township as a token of the village's high esteem and in appreciation of his bravery (*WG*, 9 June 1917). His younger brother James McCallum Sanderson (1895–1978), RFA, went over to France early in July 1915.

Sergeant James Smith (1872–1919), 6th Border, came to Grasmere from Penrith in 1907 where he worked as a joiner for T. Wilson & Sons.

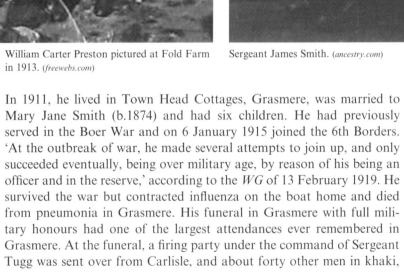

William Carter Preston pictured at Fold Farm in 1913. (*freewebs.com*)

Sergeant James Smith. (*ancestry.com*)

In 1911, he lived in Town Head Cottages, Grasmere, was married to Mary Jane Smith (b.1874) and had six children. He had previously served in the Boer War and on 6 January 1915 joined the 6th Borders. 'At the outbreak of war, he made several attempts to join up, and only succeeded eventually, being over military age, by reason of his being an officer and in the reserve,' according to the *WG* of 13 February 1919. He survived the war but contracted influenza on the boat home and died from pneumonia in Grasmere. His funeral in Grasmere with full military honours had one of the largest attendances ever remembered in Grasmere. At the funeral, a firing party under the command of Sergeant Tugg was sent over from Carlisle, and about forty other men in khaki,

James Smith's 'widow's penny', a next-of-kin memorial. (*ancestry.com*)

lately demobilized, from Grasmere and Ambleside, walked in the procession. The coffin was covered with the Union Jack and the pall-bearers – selected from among his fellow workmen – were all in khaki. The service in church and at the cemetery was said by the Reverend M.F. Peterson. At the close, three volleys were fired over the grave and the bugler sounded the Last Post. Smith is buried at St Oswald's.

Lieutenant Corporal George Edward Thompson (1895–1917), 11th Border, son of Mr and Mrs Edward Thompson of Turn Howe, Grasmere, enlisted in Kendal in 1914 and had previously been wounded during the first month of the Battle of the Somme. He was killed in action on 10 July 1917 (Western Front) following heavy bombardment by the enemy. He was witnessed trying to retire when he was brought down by the enemy machine guns. He remained officially missing in action. The enemy had been shelling the trenches of the 11th Borders all that day (Operation STRANDFEST), as well as using mustard gas for the first time which caused severe vomiting. He is remembered at St Oswald's.

Driver James Wilson (1892–1943), Army Service Corps, son of John and Ann Wilson of Highfield, Grasmere, had his report published in the *WG* on 30 September 1916:

> We have had a terrible time here for patients. I have been on at days and nights to keep it up. We have handled thousands of patients, I do not know how many, but I am sure we had a thousand outside sometimes waiting for the trains. We have some splendid RAMC men here and the Sisters have been hard at it. We have a little cemetery quite near, and since last Friday, (3 days) we have buried over 200. We were right in the centre of it and so got some of the worst cases. Last Wednesday Alf and I went off to a place near the town you named, and we stopped at an artillery ammunition dump to get a shell case when, lo and behold, I met Sid (Sydney) Fletcher, the first Grasmerian I have had the pleasure of meeting. Walt and the Sandersons are near here – only about 3 miles. Next day Tom Proctor and several more came, all lucky blighters, and the old boys have been over and done great execution. They walked over with their rifles slung over their shoulders and bombed the Huns out of it.

Gunner Sydney Fletcher (b.1894), son of George Fletcher of Town End, Grasmere, was a gardener and domestic labourer (1911 census). He married Anne McJannett, daughter of John McJannett, 2 February 1918.

Tom Fleming Wilson (1888–1916) was brought up by his grandparents at Fieldside, Grasmere. The eldest son of Tom Wilson, he was the inside manager and machinist at the works at Fieldside. He passed his examinations for the Machine Gun Corps in November 1915 and immediately enlisted in Coventry. He has the distinction of being in one of the first tanks to go onto the battlefield, on the Somme in the Battle of Flers-Courcelette on 15 September 1916, according to firsttankcrews.com. He served in tank D15 which was hit by German artillery as it crossed the German front line en route for Flers; as its crew abandoned the burning vehicle, two were killed and were hastily buried beside the tank. The remainder of the crew were wounded by enemy small-arms fire. Wilson was badly wounded in the leg; at first it was thought possible that his leg could be saved but it was later amputated and he died on 22 September 1916, a week after the legendary first tank attack on the battlefield. He was buried at Heilly Station Cemetery, Somme. His picture is in the *WG* of 30 September 1916 and he is recorded on the slate tablet inside St Oswald's. The introduction of the tank midway through the Battle of the Somme appeared to herald a new dawn warfare. At first sight, the weapon had terrorized the enemy.

CHAPTER TWELVE

We Will Not Go to War

Conscription was introduced in January 1916, targeting single men aged 18 to 41. Within a few months, conscription was rolled out for married men. Labour Peer Lord Clark (David Clark) of Windermere, author of *The Labour Movement in Westmorland* (2014), said in the House of Lords on 4 March 2013:

> There was a terrific response to the war and to patriotism. Even as late as the 1950s when I worked in Cumbria, there were still many who had fought in World War One. The interesting thing was that very few of them ever spoke about it. About 20 years later, when I was doing some research into the early years of the Labour movement in Britain, I met a great many other individuals who had taken the opposite point of view. Many had been conscientious objectors who opposed the war – not usually on religious grounds but on political grounds. Their opposition was not upheld by the tribunals and most of them ended up in prison. Indeed, they were very strange jailbirds. However, one thing was clear: both sides respected the other over the years and both groups of individuals were very brave. One must accept that.

Stanley Webb Davies (1894–1978) operated from a small workshop in New Road, Windermere from 1923 to 1960, employing about six very fine woodworkers making furniture by hand. He was the son of a prosperous mill owner in Lancashire and a committed Quaker. He served with a Friends' War Victims Relief Unit during the Great War, building wooden houses for refugees made homeless by the war in France. After his death his house, Gatesbield in Windermere, became a residential home for retired Quakers.

Hugo Harrison Jackson (1890–1918), the only child of Harrison and Lucy Jackson, was born in 1890 in Altrincham, Cheshire. The family, Quakers, then moved to Kendal. He attended Stramongate School, Kendal (founded by the Society of Friends in 1698) and became a science teacher at Sidcot School (Quaker), Devon. When war broke out in 1914, being a pacifist by religious conviction, Jackson joined the FAU and,

Hugo Harrison Jackson, aged 24.

after some initial training, went over to Belgium in November 1914. The FAU initially supplied their own vehicles and worked for the Belgian army. Subsequently they became part of the Section Sanitaire Anglaise (SSA) of the French army which then supplied their vehicles. Several units of the SSA were manned entirely by the FAU, and Jackson was part of SSA14. For some time he organized stores but pressed to be allowed to go out with the ambulances. While moving the sick and injured in Picardy along the Aisne front in May 1918, his ambulance became caught up in a rapidly shifting battlefront and was hit by a shell. The ambulance driver, Norman Edward Gripper (1898–1918), Red Cross Society, Order of St John of Jerusalem, was killed outright and Jackson did not survive the journey to the dressing station. Gripper, the son of Albert and Florence Gripper of Shrub End Road, Colchester, is buried in the joint Anglo-French Military Cemetery at Vailly in France beside his colleague. He, along with many of his SSA colleagues, both FAU and other convoys, was awarded the French Croix de Guerre.

Grave of H.H. Jackson, FAU.

Grave of N.E. Gripper, FAU.

John Francis Oliver King (1893–1924) of Ellray, Windermere, a student at Cambridge, was in the FAU from September 1914 to May 1915 and worked as an ambulance driver in Dunkirk, France. He left the FAU on medical grounds and died in 1924. His brother Philip Fell King (1897–1982), Quaker, also of Ellray and a schoolboy at Leighton Park (Quaker), Berkshire also served in the FAU as an ambulance driver. He left France for demobilization on 29 January 1919. He is buried at Troutbeck, near Windermere.

Terence Herriot O'Brien (1897–1970), Quaker, an apprentice engineer of Wraysholme, Ambleside, served in the FAU in France and returned from France due to illness on 7 February 1917. He was transferred to the Home Office scheme of Work of National Importance (WNI) and subsequently worked in agriculture.

A database of British First World War conscientious objectors (COs) compiled by Cyril Pearce, a lecturer (retired) at Leeds University who once taught the author, contains material on 17,678 COs. Twenty-nine from Kendal are listed, including Clarence Owen, No-Conscription Fellowship (NCF) Kendal Branch Secretary, of Hill Place, Oxenholme, and Hugo Harrison Jackson (above). The following served in the FAU: Sidney Rigg Allen (1886–1946), a house-painter of Sunnyholme; Thomas Card Beakbane (b.1876), Quaker, of Parr Street; Oswald Bowker (1886–1954), Quaker, a woollen mill manager of Ash Mead; Frank Holmes (b.1885), a boot and shoe operative of Romney Road; George William Holmes (b.1878), a boot and shoe operative of Romney Road; Alfred Ineson (b.1881) of Highgate; Guy Jeffreys (b.1898), Quaker, a student of Castle Green, Kendal; Hugo Amos Doyley Jones, Quaker, a bootmaker of Highgate; Ernest Jones (b.1862), Quaker, of Harwood Dale; David Stables Long (1893–1955), Quaker, a student of Skelsmergh who became a schoolteacher after the war; George William Tatham (b.1879), a printer of Nether Street; and Charles Braithwaite Wilson (1878–1970) of Bankfield. Ronald Davidson Simpson (b.1890), Quaker, a designer of Littleholme, left the FAU to join the army.

During the First World War, Kendal-born scientist Arthur Stanley Eddington (1882–1944), whose father Arthur Henry Eddington (1851–84) was headmaster of Stramongate School, Kendal and whose mother, Sarah Ann Eddington (née Shout), lived at Meadow Brow, Grasmere, began studies on Albert Einstein's general theory of relativity and on stellar structure. Arthur Eddington came from a Quaker tradition and, as a CO, avoided active war service and was able to continue his research at Cambridge. The death of physicist Henry Gwyn Jeffreys Moseley (1887–1915), who was shot and killed during the Battle of Gallipoli on 10 August 1915, highlighted debate around the neglect of science.

Bedrooms in Hawkshead for newly-released COs

Following the Great War, the parents of the historian Alan John Percivale 'A.J.P.' Taylor (1906–90), Percy Lees Taylor (1874–1940) and Constance/Connie, either owned or rented a holiday cottage in Hawkshead. In the summer of 1919, the Taylors gave holidays to a stream of COs newly-released from prison and selected by Preston solicitor William Henry (Harry) Thompson (1885–1947) who was imprisoned as a CO in 1916 and spent the rest of the war in various prisons (*A.J.P. Taylor: Radical Historian of Europe*, C.J. Wrigley, 2006). According to *Troublemaker: The Life and History of A.J.P. Taylor*, Kathleen Burk, 2002), Harry was Taylor's maternal uncle and the cottage was the Minstrel's Gallery, Berkeley Square, Hawkshead. It had plenty of bedrooms. Each group stayed a fortnight and were then replaced by another group for another fortnight. Today, the Grade II listed building is known as Minstrels Gallery and is a restaurant. According to geograph.org.uk, the building was formerly listed as Crown Mitre Cottage.

Percy Taylor, a second-generation cotton merchant, and his wife, a schoolmistress, had left-wing views, which Taylor – an only child – inherited. Both his parents were pacifists who vocally opposed the First World War, and sent Taylor to Bootham School in York, a Quaker school, as a way of protesting against the war. Various national politicians of the Left stayed at the Taylors' house in Preston, to which they moved in 1919, and Taylor spent much of his time in the company of adults. In 1924, Taylor went to Oriel College, Oxford to study modern

The Minstrels Gallery, Hawkshead (undated).

history where he lost most of his northern accent, according to *Trouble-maker: The Life and History of A.J.P. Taylor*. There is a blue plaque on the house where Taylor lived: 17 Rose Terrace (now Oakendale residential care home), Ashton-on-Ribble, Preston. Taylor loved the Lake District mountains. He is buried at Golders Green Crematorium, London. Constance died at St George's Hospital (Tooting, London), where she worked, of Spanish flu.

The War Memorial at Woodland
A craggy outcrop of rock on Green Moor, Woodland, near Coniston, is engraved with a series of six initials and the name A. Boosey. The initials are H.S., W.R.S., T.S., C.H., M.C. (G.?) and R.H. A short inscription accompanies them: 'CON OBJECTORS 1916'. All the COs who carved their names into that rock were members of either the British Socialist Party (a Marxist political organization established in 1911) or the Socialist Labour Party; not a Quaker among them. However, what were they doing in Woodland, a hamlet that at the time had a railway station on the branch to Coniston, in 1916?

CHAPTER THIRTEEN

Landowners and Gentry Remembered

In the pre-1914 world, success was still apt to be measured in terms of property, specifically a country house. However, the cost of war, death duties and the burden of income tax forced many families to sell their stately homes after the First World War, and many of the sons had died in the war, so there were fewer people to inherit such houses. The war also brought greater recognition to the 'common man'. Grand mansions around Lake Windermere – which is 10 miles in length – include Blackwell, Brathay Hall, Graythwaite Hall, Holehird House, Rusland Hall and Wanlass Howe. The Bigland Hall estate is situated between the foot of Windermere and the head of the valley of Cartmel. Rydal Hall is in the village of Rydal between Ambleside and Grasmere.

Bigland Hall

The action at Festubert on 15 June 1915 marked the end of the male line for the aristocratic family of Bigland. Second Lieutenant George Braddyll Bigland (1891–1915), 1/4th KO, who proceeded overseas on 3 May 1915, was killed in action near Rue d'Ouvert at the age of 23. He was killed in the fire trench before the advance commenced. Captain William Garencieres Pearson (1883–1963), son of Henry Garencieres Pearson and Margaret Agnes Butler (who both died in Barrow), followed up in the attack but was hit by shrapnel. He was eventually picked up by the Germans and taken prisoner. George Braddyll Bigland was the only son and heir of Editha Blanch Hinde Bigland of Bigland Brow, Backbarrow and the late squire, George Bigland. George Braddyll Bigland had been known as the 'Soldier-Squire'. Although the Bigland Hall estate was not a large one, the family of Bigland was one of the most ancient in the north. George Braddyll Bigland was the last of his line, with ancestors who for the past 1,000 years had served as soldiers. Another notable member of the family, Edward Bigland (1620–1704), was a sergeant-at-law and Member of Parliament for Nottingham

George Braddyll Bigland by Charles Braithwaite, painted 1915. *(IWM)*

during Oliver Cromwell's time. Today, Cartmel Priory Church and Kendal Church still contain memorials belonging to members of the Bigland family.

Blackwell

There is a bronze plaque with regimental crest above and the family crest below at Holy Trinity Church, Winster, Windermere to Captain Joseph Holt (1881–1915), 6th Manchester Regiment, of the fine villa of Blackwell (now an Arts & Crafts museum).

Blackwell was used in the 1940s by a girls' school evacuated from Liverpool in wartime.

Joseph Holt, a member of the Royal Windermere Yacht Club, was born in Cheetham, Manchester, the second eldest of the five children of Sir Edward Holt (1849–1928) and his wife Elizabeth Brooks. Sir Edward, who served as Lord Mayor of Manchester in 1908, had inherited a brewing company from his father. Joseph Holt was educated at Rugby and came up to Christ Church, Oxford in 1900. After Oxford, he returned to Prestwich to work in the family business. He was in the Territorials of the Manchester Regiment and was mobilized at the outbreak of war with the rank of captain in the 6th Manchester Regiment, serving in Egypt and Turkey. He was killed at Gallipoli. He has no known grave and his name is on Panel 158 to 170 of the Helles Memorial, Gallipoli, Turkey.

Braithwaite Fold

Wealthy tin-plate merchant Edmund Littler Johnson settled at Braithwaite Fold, a 1700 house (now a campsite), in 1909. Edmund Johnson (d.1918), his eldest child, enlisted on 4 September 1914 as Private 33637 with the Public Schools Battalion of the Middlesex Regiment (he is on the Rugby School register). He trained at various army camps in England. In May 1915, he was discharged from military service with signs of tuberculous pleurisy. When his battalion was sent to Boulogne on 17 November 1915, he was unable to join them. Later, with his health restored and keen to serve abroad, he re-enlisted as Private G/40280 with the 1st Battalion of the Queen's (Royal West Surrey Regiment). He fought with them on the Western Front until he was killed in action on 12 April 1918. He is remembered with honour on the Ploegsteert Memorial to the Missing in Belgium.

Brathay Hall

The prosperous London silk mercer Giles Redmayne (1792–1857) bought Brathay Hall, an eighteenth-century mansion, in 1833 and in 1836 built Holy Trinity Church (Brathay Church) at Skelwith. Gunner Giles Blomfield Redmayne (1885–1917), Royal Field Artillery, son of the benefactors of Brathay Hall, died of pneumonia while on leave. He was educated at Uppingham School, is named on the Brathay memorial cross and is buried in Brathay churchyard. He had been awarded the Military Cross for conspicuous bravery in the trenches.

Finsthwaite House

Grade II listed Finsthwaite House to the east of Lake Windermere was the residence of aristocrat Major General Thomas William Sneyd (1837–1918), pronounced Sneed, whose family home was Basford Hall, Staffordshire. (References have been found to him living at Finsthwaite House in 1894, 1905 and 1911.) He commanded the Queen's Bays from 1877 to 1881. His son and only child Captain Thomas Humphrey Sneyd (1882–1914), 4th Battalion Lancashire Fusiliers, was killed in action at Ploegsteert on 2 November 1914, buried at Ploegsteert and re-interred at Messines Ridge British Cemetery, Belgium. His battlefield cross, made by the men of his regiment, is at St Edward's Church, Cheddleton, Staffordshire. Averil Marion Anne Scott-Moncrieff, who died in March 2006, was the daughter and only child of Thomas Humphrey Sneyd and Phoebe Marianne Brodie. Phoebe married, secondly, Alfred Stratford Dugdale (1882–1974) on 25 August 1925. There may be a link to former Prime Minister David Cameron: ladies' man and war hero Sir William Stratford Dugdale, who was awarded a Military Cross in 1943 and died in 2014 aged 92, was his maternal uncle.

Graythwaite Hall

The Sandys family own the 2,000-hectare Graythwaite Hall estate. One of the more famous members of the family was Edwin Sandys, who was Archbishop of York (1576–88) and founded Hawkshead Grammar School in 1585. Captain Mervyn Keats Sandys (1884–1914), 2nd Battalion York & Lancaster Regiment, of Graythwaite Hall, was killed in action at Le Touquet, France on 22 October 1914 and is remembered on the Ploegsteert Memorial. His twin brother Major George Owen Sandys (1884–1973) inherited the Graythwaite Hall estate in 1915. Edwin Sandys built the Sandys Chapel inside Hawkshead Church in 1585 to the memory of his parents and it is still used by the Sandys family.

Grizedale Hall

Grizedale Hall was rebuilt in 1905 by Harold Brocklebank (1853–1936), a wealthy Liverpool-based merchant and shipping magnate. Harold Arthur Brocklebank (1889–1944) of Grizedale Hall, son of Harold Brocklebank and Mary Ellen Brogden, gained the rank of captain in the service of the 4th Battalion, Royal Lancaster Regiment, according to thepeerage.com. He had been reported wounded and missing at the Third Battle of Ypres in August 1917. Captain Thomas Geoffrey Brocklebank (d.1916), elder son, fell in action in France near Maricourt on 8 August 1916. There is a memorial to him – a wooden board set within a larger richly-carved board – at All Saints Church, Satter-thwaite. He was educated at Eton and Oxford. For a time, he was in a southern regiment of Volunteer Artillery. On joining the ship-owning firm of Brocklebank in Liverpool, he transferred to the West Lancashire (Howitzer) Brigade (TF), with which he went to the front in the summer of 1915.

During the Second World War, Grizedale Hall became No. 1 PoW camp to hold German officers – it could take 300 prisoners – and was pulled down in 1957. A well-known prisoner was Otto Kretschmer

A scene from the film *The One That Got Away* (1957).

(1912–98), Germany's most successful U-boat captain of the war until his capture.

Just out of curiosity, the image on the previous page is taken from the film *The One That Got Away*, filmed in the 1950s and relating to the tale of Oberleutnant Von Werra (d.1941), a Luftwaffe pilot from an aristocratic German family who made an attempted escape from Grizedale Hall on 10 October 1940.

High Borrans

High Borrans estate (incorporating the existing farm buildings) was built in the 1880s by Robert Holt, a wealthy cotton trader from Liverpool, as a summer and sporting estate for his family and guests. Barbara, his daughter-in-law, described living there during the Great War, going with her mother to sew bandages down at a depot in Windermere and gathering sphagnum moss to be dried and used for dressings for soldiers wounded in the war. They also collected wild plants that could be used for medicinal purposes: coltsfoot for bronchial troubles, foxglove for heart conditions and broom tips for kidney complaints. She died in 1981.

Holehird House

Victorian mansion Holehird House, located off the Windermere to Troutbeck road, was owned by William Grimble Groves (1848–1927) of Manchester brewery Groves & Whitnall, and working-class men from the estate served in the armed forces. In an isolated part of the estate there is a memorial stone to Cobby, one of the estate's horses that was conscripted into the war effort in 1914/16. The company also had to hand over most of its lorries during the Great War. William Grimble Groves and his wife Eliza Anne (née Leigh) had two children, Edith Mary and Henry Leigh. Henry Leigh Groves (1881–1968) gave the whole Holehird estate (500 acres, house, Holefield Farm and cottages) to Westmorland County Council in 1945 for the benefit of the people of the county. Today, the grounds of the estate are administered by Cumbria County Council and the house is leased as a nursing home (page 104).

Regarding Cobby the horse, an interesting postscript appeared in the *Wigton Advertiser* of 10 May 1919: 'Army Horses – 88,772 have been sold back to Civilian use for £3,320,028 – an average of £37/7/11, also 2,220 mules for £42,225 – average of £19/3/4 [a paraphrase].' As the army had either conscripted the horses or had been given them at the start of the war, it would appear that they made a considerable profit!

The Groves kept servants at Holehird; the cottages on the estate were for estate servants. On 19 October 1908, there was an advert in the *Yorkshire Post and Leeds Intelligencer* for a nurse for a baby. The address

Holehird Cheshire Home for disabled adults in Windermere. (*Lakes Christian Centre*)

given was Mrs McQueen, c/o Mrs Grove, Holehird. They had a gardener, Robert Edwin Robertshaw (1850–1916) of Holehird Lodge, whose death in 1916 aged 66 was not war-related; housemaids Eleanor Clark (b.1880) who was born in Cheshire, Martha Thompson Horsfield (b.1876) who was born in Dodworth, Yorkshire, Mary Earl (b.1883) who was born in Carlisle and Margaret Hughes (b.1860) who was born in Wales; Annie Whitwell (b.1867), a cook who was born in York; Williamena McKirer (1864–1950), a waitress (domestic) who was born in Scotland; Catherine Scott (b.1894), a kitchen maid who was born in Windermere; and Sarah Roberts (b.1863), a sewing maid who was born in Wales.

Visitors included the Potter family, who rented the house for the two summers of 1889 and 1895, and garden designer Thomas Mawson. Mawson lived in Windermere and designed Holehird, Graythwaite Hall, Langdale Chase, Brockhole, Holker Hall and Rydal Hall gardens among others in the district. He also set up Westfield War Memorial Village (see page 172). James Radcliffe Mawson (d.1915), 1st/5th KO, one of his nine children, was born in Windermere, enlisted in Lancaster and was about to study at the École des Beaux-Arts, Paris. He died of wounds on 24 April 1915 (Western Front). Thomas Mawson's eldest son, Edward Prentice Mawson (1885–1954), born in Ambleside and educated at Windermere Grammar School, was unable to serve in the forces due to health issues but worked in munitions for most of the war. On 5 August 1917 (orthodox calendar, which is twelve days behind the western calendar), there was the Great Fire of Thessaloniki, Greece, which burned down most of the city. Within a week, the government was inviting a worldwide competition to rebuild the city. Mawson senior entered a bid and wanted to send Edward to supervise the work. However, it took him twelve weeks to get Edward freed from his munitions employment, a delay that lost him a good part of the work, although he still played a material part in the rebuilding. Notable works of the family architectural practice include London County Council's St Helier Estate (1934).

Also Dorothy, Thomas's daughter, lost her sweetheart at the very end of the war: he eventually succumbed to wounds from which she had done so much to nurse him back to health.

Private Edward Goodier (1892–1915), Canadian Infantry, born in Northwich, Cheshire, had worked at Holehird and then emigrated to Canada. He arrived at Halifax, Nova Scotia on 11 April 1914 on the *Empress of Britain*. The passenger list is unusually good as it said he was going to St Thomas, Ontario (which is where he enlisted) to work as a gardener on a fruit farm, and had been a gardener for sixteen years. He was also 'British bonus paid'. The bonus was paid to the shipping company for taking people with important skills such as farmers or gardeners, but it would not have been paid if he had said he was going to work in a car factory (he has been listed as a car-builder). Effectively the bonus was a subsidy on the fare. His married brother, John Henry Goodier (d.1944), was already living in St Thomas, having arrived in 1912. From Edward's army papers, we know he was having $2 a month of his pay remitted to John at 128 Balaclava Street, St Thomas. John also enlisted in 1915 and survived the war. Edward was killed in action on 24 November 1915 and buried at Ridge Wood Military Cemetery, Belgium. There is an unusually detailed casualty card:

> ... at about 6.30pm in the evening he was in the trenches in the vicinity of Messines when he was struck by an enemy rifle bullet about two inches above the heart. He died within about thirty minutes without regaining consciousness. Two of his comrades were with him and gave all possible assistance.

A family history of James Grimble Groves (1854–1914), brother of William Grimble Groves, by his second son Keith Grimble Groves (1887–1979) with details of the First World War service of six members of the family is at Cumbria Archive Centre, Kendal:

> William Peer Groves (1878–1946) in 1914 enlisted in Royal Naval Air Service (RNAS), the air arm of the Royal Navy (RN). He was decorated with French Legion of Honour for work at Dunkirk in command of the sausage balloon section. A sausage balloon was a

small non-rigid airship used for observation or as a barrage balloon. Robert Marsland Groves (1880–1920) entered the RN in 1894. When World War One broke out, he was Flag Commander to the Commander-in-Chief, Mediterranean Fleet. He then joined the RNAS aged 33. He was First Commander of the Naval Forces at Dunkirk, where he flew every known type of aeroplane. He became Deputy Chief of Air Staff on 1 April 1918 when the RNAS and RFC were merged into the RAF. He held the ranks of Brigadier General, Air Commodore and Captain RN and was awarded the CB, DSO, AFC, Officier de la Légion d'Honneur and American AF Cross, and was mentioned in despatches. In September 1919, he was appointed to command RAF in Egypt and the Middle East. He was killed on 27 May 1920 when his Bristol fighter stalled soon after take-off and crashed into the ground. He was buried at Cairo Military Cemetery.

James Douglas Groves (1882–1960) emigrated to Canada in 1910 but returned to England when war broke out and joined the Derbyshire Yeomanry. He was severely wounded as a company commander at the Battle of Lens and Mentioned in Despatches. He served the rest of the war in England as a captain. Eric Marsland Groves (1884–1949) joined the RN and was one of the first submariners serving in *A9* on 14 July 1908 when there was a fault with the petrol supply. Her crew, six men in total, was rescued unconscious from the fumes. Lieutenant Groves managed to reach the engines and stop them by turning off the supply of petrol. He was invalided out of the RN and did Red Cross voluntary work in the First World War. He died on 28 July 1949 and his ashes were taken in a submarine from Portsmouth to Spithead to be buried at sea, in recognition of his bravery.

Keith Grimble Groves joined the Inns of Court Regiment on 4 August 1914 and was soon promoted to corporal, then sergeant. He was commissioned in 2/17th London Regiment in September 1914. He served at Vimy Ridge, Salonika and Palestine and was Mentioned in Despatches in November 1916. Later, he was seconded for Intelligence work at Jaffa and later Cairo where he acted as prosecutor in a war crimes case. His son Louis died in a flying accident in the Second World War. Lieutenant Commander Leslie Gordon Grimble Groves (1892–1947) entered the RN in 1905, took part in the Battle of Jutland (1916) serving aboard a light cruiser; soon after he joined the RNAS and was adjutant of the balloon section at Capel, Folkestone.

The Battle of Jutland was a naval battle from 31 May to 1 June 1916. Fourteen British and eleven German ships were sunk. HMS *Queen Mary* was sunk in the Battle of Jutland and her wreck discovered in 1991 on the bed of the North Sea. The remains of the *Queen Mary* are designated as a protected place under the Protection of Military Remains Act 1986 as it is the grave of the 1,266 officers and men who were lost. Eighteen survivors were picked up by the destroyers HMS *Laurel*, HMS *Petard* and HMS *Tipperary*, and two by the Germans (Wikipedia). HMS *Caroline* is the last survivor of the Battle of Jutland still afloat. The ship, moored in Belfast, is being transformed into a heritage visitor attraction.

Rusland Hall

Second Lieutenant Myles Falcon Downes Archibald (1898–1961) of Rusland Hall served in the Royal Field Artillery (RFA) in the Great War before continuing his education at Leeds University and becoming a barrister. A letter from the War Office dated 30 May 1918 said: 'He has never served overseas and is only fit for sedentary work. I have no use for him here.' The reasons were medical. He inherited Rusland Hall from his father Charles Falcon Archibald in 1936 but had no use for it. The Towers School, Saltburn, Cleveland was evacuated to Rusland Hall during the Second World War.

There is a brass plaque with a wooden background above the organ in St Paul's church, Rusland to Lieutenant John Arnold Archibald (1890–1918), cousin of Charles Falcon Archibald of Rusland Hall. John Arnold Archibald, 11th Infantry Battalion, Australian army, was a teacher born in New South Wales. (He is not on the main church memorial, a wooden-framed ROH.) He initially enlisted as a private on 17 August 1914 and left Perth, Australia on *Ascanius*, an Australian Expeditionary Force (AEF) troopship completed in Belfast in 1910, along with his future brother-in-law Samuel Jackson, bound for Egypt. He was present at the landing at Gallipoli on 25 April 1915, where he was wounded that day and evacuated to Valletta in Malta. He recovered and returned to the field to resume the fight. He was wounded a number of times in the fighting and also underwent periods of sickness when he had to be evacuated, sometimes to England and sometimes remaining in France. He was severely wounded in the head by an enemy bomb on 24 September 1918 in the vicinity of Roisel, northern France. He was taken to the M Dressing Station (2nd Australian Field Ambulance) and died shortly after admission.

He was buried at Tincourt New British Cemetery, Somme (Tincourt became a centre for Casualty Training Stations). In 1967, John Arnold Archibald's sister Alice Jackson, also a teacher, applied for the Gallipoli War Medal and citation for him as she was the only surviving member of that generation of the Archibald family.

Rydal Hall

Sir Thomas le Fleming and his family built the first Rydal Hall at St John's Knott in 1409 (the small mound and wood next to the entrance of the Ambleside cricket club on the A591). In 1600, William Fleming (the 'le' prefix being dropped during the Tudor wars with France) built the hall on the present site. The Kelland and le Fleming families emigrated to New Zealand in 1865 (National Library of New Zealand). There is an interesting piece in the *Carlisle Journal* of 1 June 1923 about Rydal Hall being the rented summer home of the queen of The Netherlands.

William Kelland le Fleming (1887–1918) was the son of Sir William Hudleston le Fleming and Martha le Fleming (née Kelland). He fought in the First World War with the New Zealand Rifles and died on active service in 1918. His brother Sir Frank Thomas le Fleming (1888–1971) fought in the First World War with the New Zealand Expeditionary Force. Rydal Hall went into mutual ownership and the Diocese of Carlisle purchased the freehold in 1970.

Wanlass Howe

Second Lieutenant Reginald Squarey MacIver (1892–1916), Lancashire Fusiliers, was killed leading his platoon into action on 1 July 1916 and is buried at Sucrerie Military Cemetery, Colincamps, France. MacIver, born in Ambleside and educated at Shrewsbury and Oxford University, was the tenth of the eleven children (five girls, six boys) of David MacIver (1840–1907), a steamship owner and Conservative politician, and Edith Squarey MacIver (1853–1940) of Birkenhead. Widow Edith lived at Wanlass Howe (now called Ambleside Park), Ambleside, where she died aged 86.

Reginald Squarey MacIver is commemorated on the Great War memorial at Ambleside with his brother Captain Andrew Tucker Squarey MacIver (1878–1915), born in Ambleside, who was killed in April 1915. Robert Rankin MacIver (1869–1915), a brother by their father's first marriage to Anne Rankin (1842–69), was also killed. Robert Rankin MacIver, who died on 11 September 1915, was born at Rothay Bank, Ambleside and is buried at Ration Farm Military Cemetery, France where 1,313 Commonwealth servicemen of the Great War are buried or commemorated.

In July 1920, Edith set out to visit the graves of her two sons and a stepson (above). She was accompanied by Albert, the chauffeur, her son Alan Squarey MacIver (1894–1976, born in Ambleside), 20th Lancashire Fusiliers, and Hugh 'Cherry' Sanderson. The first visitors to the battlefields, initially an expensive and complicated business, were gentry who had the resources to make the journey.

There is a brass plaque at St Margaret's Church, Low Wray to Andrew Tucker Squarey MacIver, and a brass plaque to Second Lieutenant Robert Troutbeck MacIver (d.1915), 1st Battalion Royal Scots, who was killed in action on 11 September 1915 and buried near Armentières, Flanders. There is also a brass plaque to Reginald Squarey MacIver. Robert Troutbeck MacIver was the son of Maude C. Sanderson (formerly MacIver) of 12 Mulberry Walk, Chelsea and the late Robert Rankin MacIver. He was born at Rothay Bank, Ambleside and is buried at Ration Farm Military Cemetery.

Barons Borwick of Hawkshead

Baron Borwick of Hawkshead in the County of Lancaster is a title created in 1922 for the businessman Sir Robert Hudson Borwick (1845–1936). He was chairman of George Borwick & Sons, founded in 1842 by George Borwick, manufacturers of baking and custard powders.

His son Robert Geoffrey Borwick (1886–1961), 3rd Baron Borwick, educated at Eton and the Royal Military College, Sandhurst, gained the rank of lieutenant in the service of the Royal Field Artillery. He fought in the First World War, gaining the rank of lieutenant in the service of the 20th Hussars, a cavalry regiment of the British army, and gaining the rank of captain in the service of the Hertfordshire Regiment.

His son James Hugh Myles (Robert) Borwick, 4th Baron Borwick, was born in 1917 in Wiltshire, was awarded the Military Cross in 1945 and died in 2007. Victoria Borwick, Baroness Borwick (née Poore), who married James (Jamie) Borwick, 5th Baron Borwick, in 1981, serves as MP for Kensington (as of 2016) and was Deputy Mayor of London (2012 to 2015).

Why Hawkshead? Jamie Borwick – Sir James Borwick, Bt of Eden Lacy – sent the author the following information:

> As I understand it, the Borwick family lived not in the village of Borwick (8 miles north of Lancaster) but in Eden Lacy (Penrith). George Borwick married a girl from Hawkshead, I'm told, and received as a dowry the recipe for the Borwick's Baking Powder so that when he, or his son, got the peerage they took Hawkshead as the title. I believe he retired to the south of France and there among other things collected musical instruments, which is why there is in existence the Lord Borwick Stradivarius.

Eden Lacy Lodge was acquired by Robert Hudson Borwick at the turn of the last century (essentially a one-bedroom bungalow).

CHAPTER FOURTEEN

Railways and Railwaymen Remembered

One hour after war was declared, the government took over the railways and kept control until 15 August 1921. The first major task was the mobilization of the armed forces. Another major role for the country's railways was in bringing and taking goods from munitions factories. An instruction was issued in February 1915 that railwaymen were not to be accepted into the armed forces without a signed certificate from their local management effectively agreeing to their volunteering for service. Nevertheless, by the first anniversary of the start of the war, well over 10 per cent of those who were railwaymen in August 1914 were now to be found in the army or navy.

By October 1916, the railways nationally had released 119,600 men for military service but about as many men had also left for other essential work, including the manufacture of munitions; in all over 40 per cent of their pre-war staff (*Railwaymen of Cumbria Remembered*). By Armistice Day, 184,475 men from the railway companies had entered the armed forces, equal to 49 per cent of the number of railwaymen of military age (18 to 45) on 4 August 1918.

Windermere station memorial
The Kendal & Windermere Railway was leased in perpetuity to the Lancaster & Carlisle Railway (L&CR) in 1858; the following year, the L&CR was leased to the London & North Western Railway (LNWR). A renewed attempt to extend the Windermere branch line to Ambleside attracted a lot of local support and reached Parliament in 1887. It was opposed on aesthetic grounds but failed because of its financial short-comings. On 14 August 1914, the summer services on the line were suspended and replaced by the winter timetable.

There is a memorial, unveiled on 6 September 2014, at Windermere station in the external waiting room in memory of LNWR employee Lance Corporal Alfred King (d.1916), 7th Battalion, King's Own

Chaplain Reverend Richard Cook, one of twenty-two railway vicars across the country, with some of the attendees at Windermere station for the dedication of a plaque (6 September 2014). (*Railway Mission*)

Yorkshire Light Infantry, who died on 19 September 1916. The inscription reads as follows: '1914–1918 / WW1 / In Memory of / Lance Corporal A. King / who worked as a Clerk / at this Station / and gave his life for us / First Transpennine Express.'

King, son of William Johnstone King and Sarah King of Penny Bridge, is remembered on the memorials in Penny Bridge Church, Tottlebank Baptist Church in the Furness Fells west of Haverthwaite, and Ulverston Victoria High School. The school magazine of Christmas 1919 describes the unveiling of the Ulverston Victoria High School memorial by Lord Richard Cavendish of Holker on 12 December 1919 as a 'solemnly-impressive ceremony'.

Lance Corporal Richard Arthur Crayston (1894–1914), 12th Lancers, who was born in Kirkby Lonsdale and whose family was living in Willow Lane, Lancaster in 1911, worked as an assistant at Wyman's book stall at Windermere railway station. He was killed on 12 October 1914 and is buried at Kemmel, Belgium. His brother Reginald Walls Crayston (1898–1917), Border, was shot by a sniper on the morning of 22 August 1917 and died instantly.

The Club Train ran during the war
In 1905, the Club Train began running to Manchester, providing special accommodation with armchairs and other comforts for the leading

Manchester businessmen whose homes were in Windermere. W.L. Harris in *Recollections of Oxenholme* states that the 8.30am Windermere to Manchester and return, the Club Train, ran during the First World War. The war did affect the working in that 'Oxenholme men in 1915 lost the turn to Preston men.' This may mean that engines and crews were being used differently. To 'lose a turn' also meant that a particular engine shed had one less duty to perform, so their shed had less work to do. Often, though, they gained other work to replace that lost. If there was no replacement work it could lead to a reduction of the workforce. Periodic switches of duty were not uncommon at the time. The Club Train ceased running in 1966.

Furness Railway

The Furness line linked with LNWR at Carnforth. The Furness Railway's War Memorial is located at Barrow railway station. It was unveiled by Victor Christian William Cavendish, 9th Duke of Devonshire, on 16 October 1921. Some 515 employees of the Furness Railway entered the armed forces; 68 names are commemorated, including Private Richard Moreton (d.1918), 1/4th KO. He was born in Windermere, lived in Barrow and worked as a clerk in the goods manager's office at Barrow station. He died on 9 April 1918 and is buried at Vieille-Chapelle New Military Cemetery, France. The war memorial tablet at Barrow Central station was damaged when the station was destroyed during the bombing of Barrow in May 1941. The memorial survives, bearing its scars, in the booking hall of the station as rebuilt c.1960.

Cockermouth, Keswick & Penrith Railway

From the Cockermouth, Keswick and Penrith railway (CK & PR), thirty-nine men signed up and seven names are commemorated on the CK & PR memorial in County Square, Keswick. One of these is Private John Dixon Gibson (d.1918), 2nd/4th Border, a platelayer on the CK & PR. Gibson, the son of John and Isabella Gibson of 32 Oak Street, Windermere, died on 29 July 1918 and is buried at the Tehran War Cemetery, Iran. Lance Sergeant William Notman (1890–1916), 4th Border, of Keswick was a yardsman at Troutbeck, 3 miles north of Windermere (*Railwaymen of Cumbria Remembered*).

CHAPTER FIFTEEN

War Memorials: Windermere Cenotaph

Civic memorials to those lost in the Great War are usually straight-forward to locate as they were generally erected in prominent places. Additional memorials are also located in churches, and yet more in buildings that may not be readily accessible to the public. There are also war memorials that have now fallen into disuse and have been stored away, so that as a result they are no longer visible; these require the most persistence to locate. Not everyone who lost a relative in the First World War wanted their relative's name to appear on a memorial. One mother described in a letter, now preserved in the Lancashire Record Office, that she felt this would merely act as a reminder of her loss every time she passed it.

Windermere Cenotaph
The Windermere Cenotaph war memorial is on the corner of Lake Road/Beresford Road, and it commemorates the men who lost their lives in the First World War (131), the Second World War (44), the Korean War (1) and the Northern Ireland Troubles (1) from the combined parishes of St Martin's, St Mary's and St John's. A bench has been installed with a plaque close to the Cenotaph in memory of six soldiers of the King's Royal Rifle Corps who died on a training exercise on 20 July 1945 when their boat overturned off Cockshott Point, Glebe Road, Windermere.

According to the *WG* of May 1919, it was originally decided not to have a war memorial, so clearly minds were changed at some point. Private Leonard Close, 11th Border, Lance Corporal William Gibson, 11th Border, Private John Hartley, 11th Border, Private William Haston, 11th Border, George Christopher Prickett, 11th Border, Private George Rigg, 11th Border, and Private Joseph Willshaw, 11th Border, died on the opening day of the Battle of the Somme, 1 July 1916. Gibson (named on Cenotaph) was born and enlisted at Windermere; Hartley (not named on Cenotaph) was born in Bardsea, lived in Bowness and enlisted at

The memorial, designed by John Swallow, was unveiled on 9 November 1924 by Mrs Atkinson who lost four sons in the war. (*Courtesy of Ian Stuart Nicholson*)

Percy Machell (pictured) left one son, Roger Victor Machell (1908–84). (*thelonsdalebattalion.co.uk*)

Windermere; and Haston (named on Cenotaph) was born in Kendal and lived in Bowness. Prickett (named on Cenotaph) was born in Barrow and enlisted in Windermere. Rigg (named on Cenotaph) was born in Bowness, and Willshaw (named on Cenotaph) was born in Windermere and lived in Milnthorpe.

The most prominent of those to die on 1 July 1916 was the commanding officer of the Lonsdales, Lieutenant Colonel Percy Wilfred Machell (1862–1916) of Crackenthorpe Hall, Appleby, Cumbria. He, from the older gentry of Cumbria, is commemorated on the war memorial in St Lawrence's churchyard, Appleby. The Machell and Sandys families provided leadership in the organization of the Grasmere Sports. Lord Lonsdale attended year after year, often with a distinguished house party.

CHAPTER SIXTEEN

War Memorials:
St Martin's

St Martin's at Windermere has more memorials than any other church in Cumbria, including Carlisle Cathedral. There are a number of memorial windows in the church. There is also a quite amazing war memorial oak-panelled chapel, entirely furnished with articles given in memory of fallen soldiers.

Reverend Euston John Nurse (1865–1945), rector of Windermere, received an offer in January 1917 from Sir William Bower Forwood (1840–1928) of Bromborough Hall (demolished 1932), Cheshire – a wealthy businessman, politician and visitor to Windermere for more than fifty years – to build and furnish a war memorial chapel by extending the north aisle of St Martin's. He offered to sign a contract for £3,000 if the architect could find a contractor to undertake the work at that price. On 2 July 1922, the War Memorial Chapel was dedicated by the bishop of Carlisle. Within the chapel is a marble memorial tablet to those from the parish of Bowness-on-Windermere who died in the Great War, with a raised, mottled brown marble surround. The centre is adorned with a raised Maltese cross within a wreath of laurels, below which is the general commemoration. Upon a white marble tablet within the border, listed in four columns, are the names of seventy-one men who died, listed alphabetically by surname, followed by first names/initials and any decorations awarded (no ranks or units are given). Sir William, who was commodore of the Mersey and Windermere yacht clubs, is buried in the War Memorial Chapel.

Another memorial at St Martin's is the Windermere First World War ROH for those who served and returned; 432 are named. Further pages include the names and ranks of parishioners who joined the 2nd Volunteer Battalion/Border Regiment until the Military/Service Acts of 1914 and 1918 and the Volunteer Act of 1916. Page 33 lists VADs. An ROH in a church can include anyone who went to war from that place, not necessarily born there but who just happened to be living there when

Within the Memorial Chapel: a marble memorial. (*Courtesy of Ian Stuart Nicholson*)

St Martin's Church from the south. (*Wikipedia*)

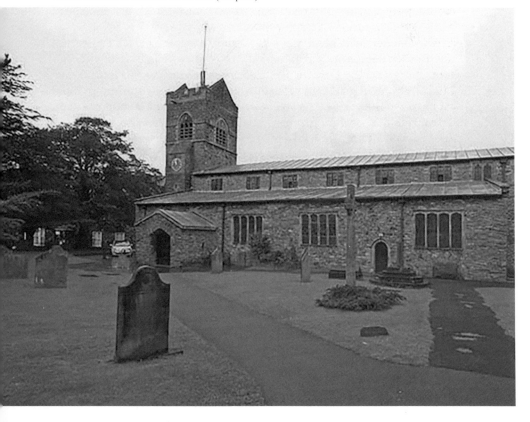

they enlisted, so they could be from anywhere. In South Westmorland, many were farm labourers who moved around so some of them are named on several ROHs and memorials.

There are forty-three names on a carved oak mural with St George and the Dragon in the centre. At St Martin's, there is a memorial window to Lance Corporal James Everett Bownass (d.1915), Princess Pat's Light Infantry. An Associate of the Royal Institute of British Architects and the son of John Titterington and Bessie Bownass of Grove House, Windermere, his attestation papers show that he joined the Canadian army in Ottawa on 24 August 1914, just a couple of weeks after the outbreak of war. He was killed in action aged 32 near Ypres on 8 May 1915. He became another of the missing and his name is engraved on the Menin Gate Memorial. The impressive window, signed by A.K. Nicholson, shows (left to right) the first depiction in England of the canonized Joan of Arc, St Martin and St George. Beneath these imposing figures are three panels depicting the ruined cathedral at Ypres, an explosion on the battlefield with a white dove rising from it – presumably the boy's soul – and an angel holding a wreath, signifying victory over death.

Another Great War memorial at St Martin's is a window depicting St Michael for the balance of justice, St George, the Patron Saint of England, and St Gabriel for Divine Power holding a Palestine Lily, made by the firm of James Powell & Sons, also known as Whitefriars Glass, 1918.

The church includes a stained-glass badges of the KO Regiment, the Border Regiment, 2nd Battalion, the Westmorland & Cumberland Yeomanry and the Loyal North Lancashire Regiment (all on the east chapel window). The north chapel window is dedicated in recognition of those who fought and served in the Great War. The Westmorland & Cumberland Yeomanry regiment was formed on the creation of the TF in April 1908 and placed under orders of the Welsh Border Mounted Brigade. It was headquartered at Penrith. On 22 September 1917, officers and men from the first line (battalion) were transferred to the 7th Borders. The second line became a cyclist battalion and the third went into the Durham Light Infantry.

There is a war diary at TNA relating to the 1/1st Cumberland & Westmorland Yeomanry from June 1916 to July 1917. The Yeomanry was (in chronological order) in Boëseghem, Isques, Thérouanne, Boëseghem, Thérouanne, Isques, Boëseghem, Essars, and then Gonnehem (25 July 1916 to 21 August 1917). On 11 August 1916 at Gonnehem, 7 officers and 150 other ranks attached to the 19th Manchester Regiment were on duty in trenches. On the same day, Major Algernon William John Clotworthy

Memorial to Lance Corporal James Everett Bownass. (*cumbrianwarmemorials*)

Skeffington, 12th Viscount Massereene and 5th Viscount Ferrard (1873–1952), a Northern Ireland politician, arrived and took over the duties of commanding officer.

There is a stained-glass window to Lieutenant John Reginald Lingard (1884–1915), 6th Manchester Regiment, who was killed in action at Suvla Bay, Gallipoli on 21 August 1915. Lingard, the only child of Thomas Dewhurst Lingard of Fellside, Windermere, is also commemorated on the Helles Memorial, Turkey. John Reginald Lingard, a member of the Royal Windermere Yacht Club, was educated at Harrow and at Trinity College, Cambridge, and he worked as a solicitor in Manchester. His father was also a solicitor. According to the *WG* of

5 September 2015, the action at Gallipoli claimed the lives of forty-five South Westmorland men in total.

The St Martin's organ was erected in 1922. The dedication reads:

THIS ORGAN WAS ERECTED / IN 1922 AND DEDICATED TO / THE WORSHIP OF GOD IN EARTH / AND IN MEMORY OF THOSE / PARISHIONERS WHO WERE CALLED / TO THE WORSHIP OF GOD IN HEAVEN / DURING THE GREAT WAR 1914–1918 / AND AS A THANKS OFFERING / FOR THOSE WHO RETURNED / TO THEIR HOMES IN PEACE.

The St Martin's Walker Credence Table is in memory of Christopher Walker (1895–1918), 16th Tank Corps, and was dedicated by his parents. He was killed in action on 19 September 1918 (Western Front). The St Martin's Waters Book Rest is in memory of Ralph Douglas Waters (1895–1917), 2nd Border, of Lake Road, Windermere, who was killed in action on 17 July 1917 (Western Front). It was dedicated by his father, brothers and sisters.

There is a memorial to Captain Edward Gerald Mucklow (1885–1918), RFC, of Elton Storrs Park, Windermere, who, after serving fourteen months in France, was accidentally killed while flying on 22 April 1918 at Stow St Mary, Essex. The cross (not on public view) was dedicated by his mother, Ada Whitehead (1854–1930), brothers and sisters.

The St Martin's Leyland Chair was dedicated by the widow of Lieutenant Herbert Edward Leyland, Royal Engineers. Leyland, who was a partner of Rigg Head slate quarry (on the way up to High Spy from Rosthwaite, Borrowdale) with his brothers, died of wounds at Westvleteren, Belgium on 17 October 1917 and is buried at Dozinghem Cemetery, Belgium. He married Mabel Maud Mildred Bownass (1884–1963) in Windermere in 1909 and in 1916 lived at Langstrath, Borrowdale, Keswick. He is also named on the Borrowdale memorials, although on the Castle Crag memorial, a dedicatory slate tablet set into a rock, the name is incorrectly spelled as Layland. Mabel ran the Borrowdale Hotel, Keswick after her father (who was the proprietor of the George Hotel, Keswick) bought it in 1926.

Leyland enlisted on 10 January 1916 and there was a memo put in with his enlistment form that he should immediately be promoted to sergeant and a second memo stating that he was a smart, intelligent quarry manager, a thoroughly competent tunneller. It was just twenty-two days before he was sent to the front, although he had two six-day spells in hospital in 1916. On 5 July 1917, he was promoted to temporary second lieutenant with the 175th Tunnelling Company. Clearly the army recognized an asset when they saw one.

Rigg Head slate quarry, where wooden-legged slater William Tyson lost his leg, was operational from the late 1880s until its closure in 1934. The range of tasks undertaken by the Royal Engineers during the war was vast, including railway construction and operation, bridge-building, barrack-building, trench maintenance and repair, searchlight operation, balloon-flying, mining and deploying gas.

The St Martin's Russell Lectern is in memory of Arthur H. Russell, 5th Border, who was killed in action at Arras on 28 April 1917. It was dedicated by his parents. There are three vases (not on public display). One is in memory of Edmund Johnson, 1st West Surrey, who was killed in action at Ypres on 12 April 1918. The second is in memory of Captain Thomas Heude Roughton, 4th Lancashire Regiment, who was killed in action at Ypres on 24 March 1918. The third is in memory of Robert Morris who served during the Great War. He died suddenly on 11 August 1937.

There is a prayer desk at the church in memory of Leslie Barwise (1889–1916) of Green Bank, Windermere, dedicated by his mother Annie Mason. He was killed in action at Delville Wood, France on 27 July 1916. A prayer desk was given to the church by the parents of Captain Maurice Tweedale (1887–1915), King's Liverpool, of Oldham. He was killed in action at Festubert on 15 May 1915.

The clergy chair is in memory of Edmund James Richardson (1899–1918), Devonshire Regiment, who was killed in action at Ste. Emilie Villers-Faucon, France on 18 September 1918. It was dedicated by his father, James B. Richardson of Cragg Brow, Windermere (now spelled Crag Brow), brothers and sisters (Frederick, Enid, Robert and Margaret). He is buried at Ste. Emilie Valley Cemetery, Villers-Faucon.

The Atkinson brothers' memorial at St Martin's, on the north wall of the War Memorial Chapel, was erected by fellow worshippers and neighbours in memory of Thomas Edward Atkinson, John Henry Atkinson, William Alfred Atkinson and Joseph Atkinson. It was previously at Carver Memorial Church, Windermere and prior to that at Congregational Church, Troutbeck Bridge. It is a bronze plaque on an oak backboard.

Eight oak pews were dedicated by the parents of Lieutenant Robert Leslie Clegg (1888–1917), Lancashire Fusiliers and RAF, who was killed in an aerial battle on 3 September 1917 near Sainte-Marie-Cappel, France. He, their only son, lived at Holbeck Ghyll and worked in cotton-spinning. In October 1914, he was gazetted to the 4th Lancashire Fusiliers and joined the 9th battalion at Gallipoli on 8 September 1915, where

Cragg Brow, Windermere. (*Public domain*)

Ste. Emilie Valley Cemetery contains 513 Commonwealth burials of the First World War, 222 of which are unidentified. (*CWGC*)

for some time he commanded a company. He transferred to the RFC and served in Egypt, latterly being a flying instructor until invalided home in May 1917. He left for the front in August 1917 and was killed while flying over the German lines.

The pews are in the Memorial Chapel. A wooden organ case with oak dedication board was dedicated by Lieutenant Colonel Sam W. Wilkinson and Jennie, his wife, as an offering of thanks for his safe return from the war and in memory of the men of his battalion, the 7th Duke of Wellingtons, who did not return.

There is a framed ROH for the dead from the First and Second World Wars at St Martin's from St John the Evangelist, Windermere (closed in 1993). It is hung in the Memorial Chapel and names thirty-two men, listed alphabetically by surname with first names, from the Great War. No ranks or units are given. The Second World War list similarly names seven men.

A copy of the St Martin's ROH to the 432 of the parish who served and returned was given to each family. Page 32 names parishioners who joined the 2nd Volunteer Battalion Border Regiment under the Military Service Acts of 1914 and 1918 and the Volunteer Act of 1916 to be sent to defend our shores in case of invasion or an attempted invasion and who received the certificate of service and the thanks of His Majesty the King: Corporal Arthur Astle, Private Charles W. Bell, Private William Clark, Private David Arnold Dunlop, Private George Evans, Private Frank E. Evans, Second Lieutenant Alfred John Greenwell, Lieutenant Henry Leigh Groves, Corporal Walter Hogg, Private Alfred Miller, Private Edward B. Martindale, Private W. Nunns, Private John Euston Nurse, Private Frank Robinson, Private George Thompson, Corporal John Clinton Trubshaw, Sergeant William James Warren, Private William Webster and Private William Woodend.

Two altar service books were given by Lieutenant Colin Deuchar and Mrs Deuchar as offerings of thanks (the church is unsure if it still has this memorial). A prayer book was given by Miss Garnett in memory of her nephews Arthur Garnett and Second Lieutenant Ralph Garnett Goddard (d.1917), Honourable Artillery Company, who was killed in action in 1917 (the church is unsure whether it still has this). There is a sanctuary prayer book in memory of Sergeant William Thompson Pearson (d.1917), 11th Border, who was killed in action at Nieuport on 10 July 1917. It was dedicated by his mother. A lectern bible was dedicated to the church by the widow of James Paterson (d.1917), 1st Border, who died of wounds in France on 30 April 1917 (the church is unsure if it still has this memorial).

An alms dish (not on public display) was given to the church in memory of Captain John Christopher Watson (d.1917), the Gordon Highlanders, by his mother. He fell while leading his men in action at Zonnebeke, Flanders on 25 September 1917 (Third Battle of Ypres). The alms dish belonged to his great-great-grandfather, Richard Watson of Calgarth Park.

Finally, the St John's ROH to the war dead (thirty-two names) is at St Martin's Church on the north wall of the war memorial chapel. St John's Church, Lake Road, Windermere was converted into assisted housing and the stained-glass memorial window placed in storage by the Diocese of Carlisle. The window with memorial plaque remembers Second Lieutenant John Miles Moss (1890–1915), Army Service Corps Mechanical Transport Company. He was the son of the Reverend John Miles Moss (1843–1928), who was the first vicar of St John's, and Mary Ethel Moss of Helm, Windermere. He died of rheumatic fever at Étretat, France on 6 September 1915 and was buried at Étretat churchyard. There is a Cavalry cross at the old St John's Church. It is also a war memorial to thirty-one men of the First World War from that parish. It doesn't quite match the St John's ROH now at St Martin's.

Étretat churchyard: Étretat is a small seaside town north of Le Havre. (*CWGC*)

CHAPTER SEVENTEEN

Further Windermere War Memorials

St Mary's Church

Reverend Reginald Mayall (1872–1944), vicar of Windermere St Mary's from 1911 to 1937, went to war as Chaplain to the Forces in 1917 and his duties were undertaken by Reverend W.J. Jones, curate of St Martin's.

There is a carved wooden mural, an ROH in memory of forty-three men of the parish who died in the Great War, at St Mary's.

James Albert Birkett (1898–1916), whose parents James and Mary lived at 7 Broad Street, Windermere, was conscripted into the Gordon Highlanders and shipped to France to fight in the trenches. He was killed at Rouen on 13 October 1916. His brother Walter Birkett (1895–1940), Border Regiment, who ran the boot and shoemaker's shop on Main Road, survived the war. However, the physical and emotional scars never really healed and he died suddenly aged 45, leaving a young son and daughter behind.

Private John Gibson (d.1916), Machine-Gun Corps, an electrician and son of William and Ellen Gibson of Alexandra Road, Windermere, is buried at Windermere (Bowness) Cemetery. He enlisted on 3 December 1915 at Leamington as Private 4543, 30th Royal Fusiliers, aged 21. He was transferred to the Machine-Gun Corps as Private 26503 on 1 March 1916. He embarked from Folkestone to Boulogne on 19 April 1916. On 28 April 1916, he was admitted to the 3rd Canadian General Hospital suffering from tonsillitis. On 6 May 1916, he was sent to England on the steamship *Aberdonia* and was admitted into the 1st London General Hospital (Section), St Bartholomew, West Smithfield, London. He died in this hospital on 15 May 1916. He had a brother, Sergeant Bruce Gibson, Royal Defence Corps, who was at the time of his brother's death stationed at the PoW Camp, Rowrah, Cockermouth. He had served in France from 24 November 1915 and survived the war.

A tablet that used to be at Old College Preparatory School, Windermere is at St Mary's Church, on the east wall. Twenty-nine old college boys fell during the First World War. The prep school on Lake Road, now a housing estate, existed from 1899 to 1966 and carried on as normal during the war.

Carver United Reformed Church

Carver United Reformed Church (URC), Lake Road, Windermere, has a First World War transcription to nine men associated with the church and Sunday School who followed the call to duty. It is likely that five of the men who died (surname Gibson) were brothers or otherwise related.

The Craig boys' preparatory school

A copy of The Craig boys' prep school, Windermere, ROH is at Kendal Archive Office. Twenty-nine names are on the memorial to the fallen: twelve for the First World War and seventeen for the second. The school was located in Lake Road, opened in 1899 and closed in 1966. Captain Thomas William Snow (b.1897) is not on the ROH but he was the son of The Craig's headmaster William Snow. He served in France from 1917 to 1919 with the 57th West Lancs Divisional Artillery and was awarded a Military Cross in 1919. He was educated at Oxford (1921) and was assistant master at The Craig from 1927 to 1932.

Windermere Golf Club and Royal Windermere Yacht Club

There are two Windermere Golf Club plaques: an ROH and a simple bronze plaque with names of the fallen only. Fifty-nine served and returned; nineteen died. The club, inaugurated in March 1891, was most successful and after eighteen months of being played as a nine-hole facility, it was extended to an eighteen-hole course. Success continued and even the Great War only slowed the club's progress. The number of visitors using the facilities in 1918 was reduced to 817 but by 1922 the number was back to 3,100.

There is a simple wooden board crest at Royal Windermere Yacht Club on Fallbarrow Road. Five members of the club gave their lives in the Great War. These include Lieutenant Thomas Storey Inglis Hall (1885–1916), 6th KO, who lived at Mereside, Windermere. Inglis Hall, son of Colonel Richard Inglis Hall, an ex-mayor of Lancaster, was killed in action in Mesopotamia. He is named on the Basra Memorial, Iraq. His wife was involved in Red Cross work in Flanders.

Windermere Grammar School

A memorial sports pavilion – including memorial tablet – was opened on 21 July 1923. The memorial tablet's current location is inside the pavilion in the grounds of St Martin & St Mary Church of England Primary

John Gibson is buried at Bowness Cemetery. (*Wikimedia*)

School, Princes Road, Windermere. The number of names for the First World War on the memorial is 216: 189 served and returned and 27 died.

Windermere Lodge of the Ancient Order of Foresters
The Ancient Order of Foresters, today trading as Foresters Friendly Society, was established in 1834, although its origins lie in a much older society named the Royal Foresters. Its first members came to recognize

they had a duty to assist their fellow men who fell into need 'as they walked through the forests of life'. This 'need' principally arose when a breadwinner fell ill, could not work and received no wages. The Windermere Ancient Order of Foresters' ROH is at Kendal Archives. There are seventy-eight names on the memorial. Seventy-seven served and returned; one man died.

Windermere Oddfellows

The Windermere branch of the Oddfellows' First World War brass plaque, in memory of twenty-six members who fell, is currently located at Kendal Archive Centre. These include Albert Ramsey Capstick (1895–1918), London Regiment, who lived in Ambleside. He was killed in action (Western Front) on 9 August 1918. James Hems (1899–1916), 1st/4th KO, lived in Ambleside and was killed in action (Western Front) on 3 August 1916. He is remembered at Thiepval. Albert Shuttleworth (1896–1916), 8th KO, was born in Millom, lived in Ambleside and had worked as a farm labourer. He died of wounds (Western Front) on 11 July 1916 and is buried at St Sever Cemetery, Rouen. His brother James Shuttleworth (1893–1916), Royal Engineers, was also born in Millom. He lived at Slack Cottage, Ambleside and had worked as a joiner apprentice. He was killed in action (Western Front) on 5 August 1916.

Fretwork War Shrine, High Wray, Windermere

This small fretwork shrine (opposite) must have been taken outside for the photo, as its usual location is on the inside face of the front wall of the village hall. The author believes that it may have lain forgotten for many years in a cupboard in High Wray village school (closed in 1931 when the building became the village hall) and only saw the light of day in recent years. It would probably prove impossible to discover who created it, though it is possible to make an informed guess.

As it was in the former village school, it may have been created by local children but the workmanship is of high quality, therefore suggesting a trained hand. Reverend Rawnsley, who moved to St Kentigern's Church, Crosthwaite, Keswick in 1883, founded Keswick's School of Industrial Art (KSIA) as an evening class in woodwork and repoussé metalwork and swiftly developed a reputation for high-quality copper and silver decorative metalwork. The outbreak of the Great War brought dramatic changes as the craftsmen enlisted and hardship reduced the demand for Arts & Crafts. In these difficult circumstances the school existed by filling a need for memorial plaques and crosses. Therefore it is not unreasonable to suggest that this small shrine was

The workmanship is of high quality. (*cumbriawarmemorials*)

created by a local person who had learned the craft of woodworking under Rawnsley. The KSIA closed in 1984.

Winster, Windermere
Designed by Mary Kynaston Watts-Jones (1879–1951), wife of Captain Hector Lloyd Watts-Jones of Canon Hey, Windermere, this memorial

cross in the Winster Valley is interesting in a number of respects. When a faculty was first applied for at the consistory court at Carlisle, it was refused with the observation that it too closely resembled a tombola. It is also slightly unusual in that the designer's name is inscribed on the base of the memorial. In general, it was a matter of principle that only the names of those who served or died should be inscribed on a cross.

Mrs Watts Jones unveiled the memorial herself in October 1920 and she is also buried beside it. Originally it was higher but some years ago the branch of a tree fell and broke the shaft, leaving the restored cross looking rather truncated. There is some thought that Mrs Watts-Jones, née Potter, was related to Beatrix Potter. A commentator on cumbrianwarmemorials.blogspot.co.uk wrote that Mary Kynaston Potter was a recognized sculptor. 'She was the daughter of Edmund Peel Potter who was the first cousin of Rupert Potter, Beatrix's father. Mary was married to Hector Watts-Jones and lived on Lake Windermere,' said Simon Potter.

Captain William Higgin Birkett of Birkett Houses, Winster, a member of the Royal Windermere Yacht Club, is commemorated by a plaque in Holy Trinity Church, Winster. On 28 October 1914, while serving with the 2nd Lancashire Fusiliers, he was wounded in the head by a shell fragment. He left the front-line trench to go to the dressing station to have his wound attended to. His men watched him walk down the road towards the Advanced Dressing Station. However, he never arrived and no trace of him has ever been found.

Windermere Methodist Church
Company Sergeant Major Charles Greenwood Dixon (1890–1919), Durham Light Infantry, died on 22 January 1919 and was buried at Dunkirk Town Cemetery, France. He was a student at St John's College, York from 1908 to 1910 and a teacher at Reid Street School, Darlington. His home town was Windermere and he is on the Wesleyan School Windermere ROH (opposite), which was in storage but has now gone on display at Windermere Methodist Church as a consequence of Ian Stuart Nicholson's hard work for the IWM. He has measured this hand-drawn memorial (see iwm.org.uk, ref. 70463), which is in the form of a scroll with the names within a laurel wreath, in a glazed wooden frame. Also named are Private James Bell (d.1918), Monmouthshire Regiment; Private Lawrence Long (1899–1918), 1/4th Yorkshire Regiment, who was killed in action on 10 April 1918 and is remembered with honour at Croix-du-Bac British Cemetery, Steenwerck; William Robinson; Private John Cavin Willshaw (1894–1918), KO; Robert Charles Willshaw (d.1917), KO, of Holly Terrace, Windermere; and George Watson Steele

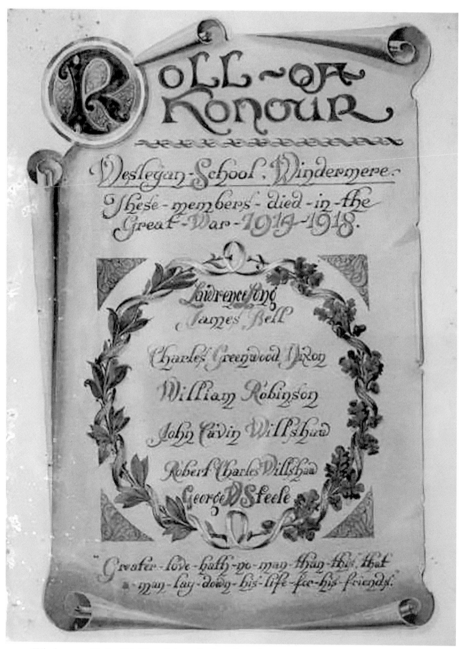

Windermere Methodist Church is at the junction of Main Road and College Road.
(*warmemorials.myfastforum*)

(1882–1916) of Hendon, London who was born in Windermere, the son of Lancelot and Mary Steele.

An unusual memorial: a tank

The presentation of a tank to Windermere took place on the afternoon of Friday, 27 February 1920. The Girl Guides and Sea Scouts provided an escort. On behalf of the War Savings Committee, the Reverend T.B.A. Saunders presented a tank and it was accepted on behalf of the council by Mr G.H. Pattinson. Windermere's tank was scrapped in 1937.

CHAPTER EIGHTEEN

War Memorials: Ambleside

The unveiling and dedication of the Ambleside War Memorial, a tall gothic cross memorial atop a rocky outcrop adjacent to St Mary's Church, took place on 6 March 1921 and was attended by Lieutenant Colonel George Gateny and the Bishop of Barrow. It was erected in memory of the men of Ambleside – sixty-eight in total – who fell during the Great War.

Private Thomas Dugdale (1894–1916), 11th Border, and Lance Corporal Richard Jackson were killed in action on 1 July 1916 (Western Front), the opening day of the Battle of the Somme. Dugdale was born and enlisted in Ambleside and Jackson was born in Ambleside.

Private Joseph Dawson (1891–1916), Canadian Infantry (Central Ontario Regiment), died on 19 September 1916. He was the son of Thomas Dawson, a slate quarryman (d.1901), and Kate Dawson of 6 Wansfell Terrace, Ambleside and is remembered on Vimy Memorial, France. It is a memorial to all Canadians who served their country in battle during the First World War.

Thomas Dugdale.

Pioneer Joseph Jackson Douthwaite, Royal Engineers, was the son of Thomas Jackson and Jane Douthwaite of 2 Rydal View, Millans Park, Ambleside. He died on 2 June 1919 and was buried at St Mary's churchyard, Ambleside. His brother Private Walter Birkbeck Douthwaite, 8th Border, was killed in action on 15 July 1916 (Western Front). He is remembered at Thiepval. Another brother Frederick Wilson Douthwaite (1894–1928), Royal Field Artillery, survived the war.

Private Frank William Hawkrigg (1892–1918), Notts & Derby Regiment, was born at Park Gates, Rydal. He was one of ten children of William and Janet Hawkrigg of Hazeldene, Green Bank, Ambleside and husband of Ruth Hawkrigg of Victoria Road, Workington. He enlisted in Kendal, was killed in action on 21 March 1918 and is remembered on the Pozières Memorial. It is likely that he died during the *Kaiserschlacht* (the 'Kaiser's Battle' or the Ludendorff Offensive), according to a contributor on 1914–1918.invisionzone.com. His name was read in the ROH at the Tower of London on 9 September 2014, together with his brother-in-law Wallace Jones (not on Ambleside), when the poppies were displayed.

Frank William Hawkrigg. (*Courtesy of his family*)

Private Albert Edwin Lamb (1886–1918), Army Service Corps, died on 3 November 1918 in Kendal and was buried at St Mary's churchyard. He was the son of Enoch and Margaret Lamb, husband of Mary Lamb (née Cordner), and lived in Ambleside (1911). Private Frank Mackereth (1888–1916), Manchester Regiment, was the son of Arthur and Mary Mackereth of Yew Tree Cottage, Ambleside. He was killed in action on 23 July 1916 (Western Front) and is on the Thiepval Memorial.

Private Albert Newby (1889–1918), RAMC, who was born in Ambleside and worked as a servant ('hotel boots') at Queen's Hotel in the centre of Ambleside (1911), enlisted at Holborn, Middlesex. He was killed by a shell at a clearing station on the Western Front on 21 March 1918.

Private Harry Salkeld (1900–1918), Manchester Regiment, the son of William and Elizabeth Salkeld of 11 Clappersgate, Ambleside, died on 24 October 1918 in Denbighshire, Wales and is buried in Brathay (Holy Trinity) churchyard. Corporal Frank Thistlethwaite (1889–1917), 7th Border, son of Thomas and Dora Thistlethwaite of 3 Lake View, The Gate, Ambleside, was killed in action on 23 April 1917 (Western Front) and is on the Arras Memorial. Corporal Bertie Avery Thomas, 4th Border, son of Annie Thomas of Westwell, Millans Park, Ambleside and the late W.H. Thomas, died of wounds on 22 November 1915 in Mesopotamia and is on the Basra Memorial. Private Harold Dudley Vity (1896–1917) was the son of John and Johanna Vity of Norwood House, Ambleside. He was killed in action on 20 September 1917 (Western Front) and is on the Tyne Cot Memorial. Private Arthur Edward Woodend (1885–1918), son of John and Mary Woodend of Holker House, Ambleside, died of wounds on 7 November 1918 (Western Front) and is buried at Kezelberg Military Cemetery, Belgium.

The death of Private Charles Flitters (1877–1915), 6th Border, of Ambleside, was reported in the *Barrow News* on 28 August 1915. He had been a soldier since 1895, was awarded two medals in the Boer War, served nine years in India and also served in the Dardanelles from 23 June 1915. He died of wounds. Private George D. Walker, 7th Border, of Ambleside died on 30 August 1915. He was formerly under-gardener at Loughrigg Brow, Ambleside. He served in France, caught a fever and died before reaching hospital.

Ambleside covered Rydal in terms of the First World War; it only has a Second World War memorial.

The King's School & Aylwin College Memorial is inside St Mary's Church. It is a wooden board, unveiled in 1952, in honour of twenty-six old boys who died in twentieth-century conflicts.

Ambleside School Old Boys

The Ambleside School Old Boys First World War memorial is a slab of rough-hewn stone set in a wall on Vicarage Road, Ambleside. There are no names on the memorial. Old boy Norman McLeod Staveley (1896–1916) from Ambleside, 8th Border, was killed in action in France on 3 July 1916 and is commemorated on the Thiepval Memorial. His brother, William McLeod Staveley, also an old boy, was a private serving with the Royal Lancaster Regiment. He fought in the Second Battle of Ypres and died on 8 May 1915.

On show in Ambleside

The Fell and Rock Climbing Club (FRCC) memorial plaque, unveiled on 8 June 1924, was placed at the summit of Great Gable Mountain and in 1926 Great Gable Memorial land was extended into the Ennerdale Valley. The memorial plaque was removed on 10 July 2013 by the Royal Engineers and a replacement plaque was installed at the summit of Great Gable in September 2013, also by the Royal Engineers, and unveiled on 10 November 2013 at a ceremony attended by John M. Barrett, Club President. The inscription is as follows:

> FELL & ROCK CLIMBING CLUB / IN GLORIOUS & HAPPY MEMORY OF THOSE / WHOSE NAMES ARE INSCRIBED BELOW / MEMBERS OF THE CLUB – WHO DIED FOR / THEIR COUNTRY IN THE EUROPEAN WAR / 1914 – 1918. THESE FELLS WERE ACQUIRED / BY THEIR FELLOW-MEMBERS & BY THEM / VESTED IN THE NATIONAL TRUST FOR / THE USE & ENJOYMENT OF THE PEOPLE / OF OUR LAND FOR ALL TIME: / [NAMES]

The old memorial was moved to the Armitt Museum, Ambleside. One of the twenty names was a B.H. Whitty. This was an error and his name was actually Whiteley; the name was corrected in 2005 but in a very obvious manner. The memorial was designed by W.G. Collingwood. The *FRCC Journal* of 1922–24 includes a detailed map of the land that was part of the memorial scheme. It is at Armitt Library in Ambleside.

The absence of practically every active member of the FRCC on war service at home or abroad caused unusual difficulty and delay in obtaining material for the November 1915 *Journal of the Fell and Rock Climbing Club of the English Lake District*. Rock-climbing in the Lake District had come to an end, except for soldiers or munitions workers on furlough. FRCC member Lieutenant Edmund Hartley (1894–1918), Lancashire Fusiliers, took part in the Battle of Arras and was wounded for a third time on 10 April 1917, a bullet passing through his left lung.

The latter part of his convalescence was spent at Broad Leys, Windermere, where he made a recovery under the care of Mrs Currer Briggs and her staff. On three occasions, he visited Langdale and climbed on Pavey Ark. February 1918 saw him once more in France. On 18 May 1918, while in command of a brigade working party at night, he was killed by a shell. Henry Laurence Slingsby (1894–1917), KO, was an FRCC member, a chemistry student and lived in Lower Allithwaite. He died of wounds on 11 August 1917. FRCC member Major John Haworth Whitworth (1879–1918), 2/6th Manchesters, married the daughter of Mr A.J. King of Elleray, Windermere. During the severe fighting at the end of March 1918, he commanded his battalion and was awarded the DSO. He died on 31 March 1918 of wounds received six days before and is buried at St Sever Cemetery, Rouen, France.

The memorial was installed on rocks around the summit and dedicated at a special service of 500 people in June 1923. One of the speakers at the dedication was Cambridge-educated climber Geoffrey Winthrop Young (1876–1958), who grew up in Berkshire, was a master at Eton from 1900 to 1905 and a poet. During the war, he was at first a war correspondent for the liberal *Daily News* but later, as a CO, was active in the FAU. On 31 August 1917, when commanding an FAU in Italy, he was severely wounded at the battle of Monte San Gabriele and lost his leg above the knee. After the war he surprised his friends by continuing to climb on a metal peg limb. His work for the *Daily News* included a book published in 1914 entitled *From the Trenches: Louvain to the Aisne, the first record of an eye-witness*, which can be downloaded for free online (317 pages).

The memorial was designed by W.G. Collingwood. His daughter Barbara modelled the relief map in Plasticene. Collingwood – W.G. as he was known – joined the Admiralty intelligence division at the outbreak of the First World War. In 1919, he returned to Coniston. He is buried near Ruskin at St Andrew's Church, Coniston, with his family. Collingwood edited a number of Ruskin's texts and published a biography of Ruskin in 1893. Ruskin died at Brantwood, Coniston in 1900. W.G.'s only son Robin George Collingwood (1889–1943) achieved eminence both as a philosopher and as a scholar of Roman Britain. During the Great War, he worked in naval intelligence before returning to academic life.

CHAPTER NINETEEN

War Memorials: Grasmere

A decorated cross of local green slate was unveiled in Recreation Park on the outskirts of the village by the Bishop of Carlisle on 15 April 1921. It is a Celtic cross and was designed by W.G. Collingwood. There are no names on the memorial.

The dedication is as follows:

In Honour of the Men
of Grasmere who
Fought and in Ever
Thankful Memory
of the Men who Died
For God For King For Home
For Freedom Peace & Right
In The Great War
1914 – 1918
1939 – 1945
[1939–1945 added post-1945]

Below this is a poem:

THE IMMORTAL DEAD
These died in war that we in peace might live
They gave their best so we our best should give
Not for themselves, for freedom home & right
They died and bid us forward to the fight
See you to it that they shall not have died in vain.

St Oswald's

There is a plain rectangular slate tablet with incised inscription inside St Oswald's Church in memory of the First World War (twenty-four names) and the Second World War (two names). In the font area, there is also an ROH. There is a brass plaque on it. It was dedicated at a ceremony on 27 March 1921. At the very bottom on its own slate tablet is Margaret Lilias Sumner (1859–1919) of Kelbarrow, Grasmere,

daughter of the late Reverend John Henry Robertson Sumner and Elizabeth Ann Sumner, and sister of Elizabeth – Lily – and Jane Henrietta
Sumner. Her grandfather John Bird Sumner (1780–1862) was Archbishop of Canterbury between 1848 and 1862.

For many years, Private John Herbert Baisbrown (1881–1918),
1st Border, of College Road, Grasmere had worked for Manchester
Corporation Water Works at Thirlmere Reservoir (which undertook the
work of Thirlmere). He signed up in the early drafts in September 1914
as a 'Kitchener Volunteer' and served in France for three years. After
serving for so long and seeing action at the Somme among other battles,
he became dangerously affected by mental illness in January 1918 and
later died aged 37.

Driver Frederick Bone (also known as Frederick Brooks),
58th Infantry Battalion, Australian army, left Melbourne on HMAT
Orsova (A67) on 1 August 1916 and disembarked at Plymouth. He spent
some time training at Codford, Wiltshire before departing for France.
He died on 6 November 1918 and, according to the CWGC, he was
buried at St Sever Cemetery Extension, Rouen, France. Before emigrat-
ing to Australia, he had lived at Under How, Grasmere with his wife
Ethel Ruth and kept a fruit shop, now Miller How Café, in Red Lion
Square, Grasmere. On the outbreak of war, the Prime Minister of
Australia, Andrew Fisher, pledged that his country would 'stand beside
Britain to help and defend her to the last man'. Overall, 416,000 Austra-
lians enlisted in the armed forces, more than one in ten of the country's
population. Around 20 per cent of the volunteers who joined the
Australian Imperial Force (AIF) in 1914 had been born in Britain.

Major John Gordon Dutton, Royal Field Artillery, was the second of
four sons of Mr and Mrs G.H. Dutton of Crag House, Grasmere who
were fighting in France. He had previously served in the Territorial
Army before moving to Chile in 1910, but returned to England in 1914
and enlisted immediately. He had been serving on the Western Front for
more than three years at the time of his death. He died of wounds on
5 April 1918 at the start of the two-day Battle of the Avre, during
German preliminary action. He was buried at Marissel French National
Cemetery.

Lieutenant Francis Rudolf Danson (1892–1915), Cheshire Regiment,
was killed on 10 August 1915 at the Dardanelles leading his men into
battle near Suvla and was buried at Sulajik. He was educated at Sedbergh and Trinity College, Oxford. He was the son of Francis Danson of
Dry Close, Grasmere, whose youngest son Captain John Raymond
Danson (1893–1976), 1/4th Battalion Cheshire Regiment, was awarded

the Military Cross (*London Gazette*, 1 January 1919). There is a plaque to Francis Rudolf Danson at Sedbergh School Chapel.

Private Henry Bowness Johnson, 11th Border, the eldest son of Mr N.B. Johnson of High Broadrayne, Grasmere, enlisted in the Lonsdales just after turning 18 in May 1915 before leaving for France on 19 December 1915. Just a few months later when leaving the trenches he was found to be suffering from measles and then pneumonia and died before his 19th birthday, on 6 April 1916 (Western Front). He was the first of three Grasmere men from the 11th Borders to die on the Western Front and was awarded the British War Medal and Victory Medal.

Before the war, Sergeant Alfred Marsden, 8th Border, was employed at the Rothay Garden Hotel, Grasmere. He was killed by a shell bursting in the middle of a working party in the support lines on 28 April 1916. A letter written by Lieutenant Dawson to Alfred Marsden's mother read:

> It is with the greatest regret that I have to inform you of the death of my platoon sergeant. He went out on fatigue duty yesterday evening, and at about 7.00pm the enemy shelled heavily, and unfortunately your son was amongst the men killed instantly. It would be consoling for you to know that he would undergo no suffering, as so many do.

There is an original battlefield cross to William Warwick Peascod (1898– 1917), 8th Border, son of William and Jemima Peascod of Island View, Grasmere, within the church. He was killed in action on 5 November 1917 and is buried at Cambrin Military Cemetery, Pas de Calais (was begun in February 1915 and used as a front-line cemetery until December 1918). He was well-known in the village for carrying the harp in the Grasmere Rushbearing.

Battlefield crosses
Makeshift graves were often marked with small wooden crosses that appear to have been the responsibility of the carpenters of the battalion. The original wooden crosses with the names of the casualties which marked their graves were offered to the families when the CWGC took over the cemeteries and erected Portland stone headstones. Everyone who was buried in the battlefield got a cross originally. However, they were often not recoverable, either because the crosses had been lost in later battles or because the graves themselves had been lost in the later battles. Little Clifton Church near Workington got seven battlefield crosses, although they asked for more, all of which went to relatives after a time in the churchyard.

Wooden crosses dating from the First World War are not as rare as people make out. However, what is rare is one bearing Graves Registration Unit (GRU) tags (Finsthwaite, see page 151).

Driver Thomas Warwick Peascod (1880–1917), Royal Field Artillery, is named on the slate plaque inside St Oswald's. The son of Isaac and Mary Peascod of Blake Syke, Grasmere, he is buried at Tyne Cot Memorial. He was married at St Oswald's in September 1916 to Roberta Alonby of Ambleside a few days before going over to France.

Private William Wilson, 8th Border, the younger son of William Wilson of Field Foot, Grasmere, worked both as a farm man and later as gardener at The Hollins, Burneside, Kendal. Private Wilson had served

The original battlefield cross from the grave of William Warwick Peascod. (*warmemorialsonline*)

Thomas Warwick Peascod was married in September 1916 to Roberta.

Cambrin Military Cemetery contains 816 burials of the First World War. (*CWGC*)

first in Egypt from December 1915 and then in France from July 1916. He was killed instantly on 27 September 1916 when a bomb hit his trench at the front line at Thiepval at the start of the Battle of Thiepval Ridge.

Great Cross Cottages for local people
Sir Frederick William Chance (1852–1932), who ran the family's textile manufacturing and printers firm in Carlisle, Ferguson Brothers (1824–1991), was a Liberal Party MP for Carlisle from 1905 to 1910 who died in 1932 at his country house in Grasmere, Lancrigg, where he had lived in retirement for several years. Sir Frederick, whose wife Mary Seton-Karr died in Carlisle in 1905, had five sons and a daughter. He commemorated his sons who fell – Captain Andrew Ferguson Chance (1882–1915) and Lieutenant Colonel Edward Seton Chance (1881–1918) – by building two cottages for local people: Great Cross Cottages, Grasmere. There are plaques on what are now 7 and 8 Great Cross Cottages, just simple slate ones. However, they are classified as war memorials and read:

No. 7 – IN MEM / ESC / MAY 29, 1918
No. 8 – IN MEM / AFC / OCT 13, 1915

This was the basis for the Great Cross Trust charity based in Ambleside. Today, Great Cross Trust owns and manages the letting of eleven affordable houses in Grasmere. The Chance brothers are also on the memorial of Holy Trinity Church, Carlisle.

Charterhouse-educated Edward Seton Chance, 2nd Dragoon Guards (Queen's Bays), who lived in Grasmere, died at Aisne, France on 29 May 1918 and is on the Soissons Memorial, Aisne. He is also on the St Oswald's memorial, there is a bronze plaque memorial to him at St James's Church, Carlisle and he is on the Trinity College Oxford ROH. Repton and Charterhouse-educated Andrew Ferguson Chance (1882–1915), Royal Field Artillery, served in Ireland and India from 1911 to 1914. When the Great War began, he volunteered for service with the Indian Expeditionary Service and arrived in France in November 1914. He was killed in action by a shell on 3 October 1915 while on duty near the town of Béthune, northern France, and there is a bronze plaque memorial to him at St James's Church, Carlisle.

The *West Cumberland Times* reported on 2 September 1916:

> The government of the Cumberland Infirmary at Carlisle on Wednesday decided to invest in 5% Exchequer Bonds £1,000 which has been received from the relatives of the late Captain A.F. Chance for the endowment of a bed in the institution to his memory. The bed will be placed in the King Edward Ward and there will be affixed to it a brass inscribed 'In memory of Captain Andrew Ferguson Chance, RFA, who laid down his life for his country in France on Sunday October 3rd 1915. This bed is dedicated by his father, brothers and sisters.'

The *Carlisle Journal* of 22 October 1920 reported:

> The secondary schools sub-committee of the CCC have framed a draft scheme for the award of the Edward Seton Chance Scholarship ... of the value of interest on a sum of £3,000 5% War Loan, being one half of £6,000 given by Sir Frederick Chance towards the establishment of a School of Chemistry in Carlisle for the benefit of the City and the County. That scheme has been postponed due to the state of the building trade, so the income is to be utilised by two scholarships, one in memory of each of his sons – one open to candidates from the county, and one to candidates from the City of Carlisle.

The two younger Chance brothers, Captain Kenneth Miles Chance (1893–1980), 6th Border, of Morton, Carlisle and Captain Frederick Selby Chance (1886–1946), 4th Border, of Homeacres, Carlisle were also in service. Oxford-educated Kenneth Miles Chance suffered severe wounds on 7 June 1917 in Belgium. A bullet entered the right side of his chest. He left for England on 1 July 1917 because of his wound and was granted leave on 18 December 1917. Their brother Sir Robert Christopher Knight Chance (1884–1960) lived in Cummersdale, Carlisle in 1911. He was Mayor of Carlisle from 1929 to 1930 and afterwards alderman and magistrate. In 1938, he was High Sheriff of Cumberland, was knighted in 1946 and became Lord Lieutenant in 1949. In 1952, he was appointed Freeman of Carlisle. He died in December 1960 in Carlisle.

CHAPTER TWENTY

Exploring South Lakeland Memorials

❧

Blawith, Water Yeat and Nibthwaite

There is a First World War wooden board in St Luke's Church, Lowick Bridge, previously at St John the Baptist Church, Blawith (closed in 2011 to become a private house) to remember nineteen men of the hamlets of Blawith, Water Yeat and Nibthwaite who served and returned.

Although not named on the board, which was created by a tradesman in Nibthwaite, the following men have local connections. Private Samuel Oliver (d.1916) of Apple Tree Helm, Blawith was killed in action on 30 December 1916. Private Daniel Muncaster (1894–1916), KO, of High Nibthwaite died in France on 11 August 1916. Private Joseph Muncaster (d.1917), Canadian Infantry, of High Nibthwaite died on 28 April 1917.

After the Great War, memorials placed within St John the Baptist Church, Blawith included a Shrigley & Hunt window bearing stock figures of St Michael and St George. On the sill of the window was a brass plaque with the names of the village dead. These memorials (which apparently had to remain in place in the new residence) were installed in 1921 after money was raised in Blawith, Water Yeat and Nibthwaite by ladies who knocked on every door. Some people gave a few shillings, one or two just a few pennies.

Brathay

Outside the entrance door to Holy Trinity Church, Brathay is a memorial cross unveiled and dedicated on 28 August 1921. There are thirteen names on the memorial. The Brathay ROH and Book of Remembrance are inside the church: fifty served and returned; eleven died. In the middle of the south wall of the church is a plain brass plaque to John Hamilton Gair (1860–1915) of Brunt How, Loughrigg, who died on 3 July 1915 in Westmorland, and his son Thomas Gair (1889–1917), Royal Field Artillery, who was killed in action near St Julien, Flanders on 9 September 1917.

The east window in the church and bronze plaque nearby were dedicated on 1 April 1917 to the memory of Captain Thomas Henry Withers Cunliffe, Lancashire Fusiliers, the only son of Robert Ellis and Helen Cunliffe. Cunliffe, who had served with his regiment since 1905, fell in action at Gurkha Bluff on the Gallipoli Peninsula, Turkey on 4 June 1915 while in charge of the machine-gun section of the battalion. He is buried in Lancashire Landing Cemetery, Turkey. His father was a solicitor at Ambleside; his home address was The Croft, Ambleside.

Burneside

The James Cropper paper mill by the River Kent in Burneside, a small village on the Windermere branch line, has made all the paper for the Royal British Legion poppies since 1978. The paper mill, which used the railway to good effect, was founded in 1845. Until 2000, James Cropper – a descendant of the original James Cropper, a Quaker merchant of Liverpool – owned a large proportion of the village; it was then sold to housing agencies. Also there is a memorial at the factory to the twenty-three workers who lost their lives in the First World War and nine in the Second World War.

Private Reuben Ellwood (1890–1917), 6th Border, son of Edward and Jane Ellwood of Skelsmergh, north of Kendal, is on the memorial. He attended Burneside School and then joined his father working for Cropper's. He volunteered in September 1914 at Carlisle and joined the Border Regiment. In October 1915, after the Battle of Loos, the *WG* reported a fellow soldier stating that 'all the Kendal men came out quite safe except poor Ellwood who got badly wounded.' He had received a bullet wound and gas poisoning but, after a period in hospital in Birmingham, he returned to the front. He died on 6 October 1917 in a casualty clearing station from multiple shell wounds received during the Battle of Poelcapelle near Ypres.

There is a wooden cross inside St Oswald's Church, Burneside – known as the Westmorland Cross – with a brass plaque for each casualty (twenty-five of them) of the Great War. Outside, there is a cross behind the west wall of the church. A plaque with names is fixed to the wall of the church behind it. There is also a new additional memorial at the church. The lychgates are dedicated to the men who lived or worked in the parish of Burneside who served their country in time of war.

Crook

There is an ROH in a wooden glazed frame in St Catherine's Church, Crook, a village located on the B5284 between Kendal and Windermere. Thirty men are named: twenty-seven of them served and returned; three

A memorial at the Cropper's factory. (*Courtesy of Cropper's*)

The James Cropper factory at Burneside Mills, 1904: the company reached its 170th year in business in 2015. (*Courtesy of Cropper's*)

This was a sketch by Charles James Cropper (1852–1924), chairman of Cropper's, of the peace celebrations in Burneside in 1919. He died as a result of a hunting accident.

Arranged by Beatrice Willink

Sketched from memory by Charles Cropper

BURNESIDE, JULY 26 1919

Village halls as war memorials: the Crook Memorial Hall Great War plaque. (*Author*)

died. The Crook Memorial Hall, a village hall where Crook Young Farmers meet every week and where folk-dancers meet, is a stone brick building and a memorial to the Great War.

Crosthwaite

Yew Tree Farm, Crosthwaite, between Windermere and Kendal, was occupied for years by the Middlebrough family. In the First World War, several sons of Thomas William and Esther Middlebrough joined the cavalry. Two of them, Gunner John Thomas Middlebrough (1894–1916), RFA, who was killed in action on 14 November 1916, and Private Christopher Pattinson Middlebrough (1897–1916), 7th Border, who died of wounds on 7 August 1916, are remembered on the Crosthwaite Brass and Westmorland Cross inside St Mary's Church. Until 1998, the cross was outside. Seventeen men are listed on the brass and cross. Private Thomas Pearson (d.1918), Machine-Gun Corps, who died in France on 21 March 1918, is only on the cross. Local legend has it that the cross was made of oak from the parish. However, it is widely believed that all Westmorland crosses were made at the same works near Kendal.

Far Sawrey

Eleven men are named on the Far Sawrey Memorial at St Peter's Church. Pioneer Gilbert Coward, Royal Engineers, of Graythwaite Hall Farm, Hawkshead was killed in action. He was formerly employed as a gamekeeper.

In the chancel at the church is a rectangular brass plaque with wooden backboard to the memory of William Mossop Fleming who was killed on 25 September 1916. He had been for many years a chorister of the church.

On the east wall of the south crossing are two Union flags. These were donated to the church in 1956 by Reverend Charles Cecil Dickson. He was a First World War chaplain with the 66th Division, 198th Brigade, 2nd East Lancashire Regiment. The large flag was loaned by him to General HQ in France to celebrate the signing of the Armistice as they were not allowed to keep a large flag. It was also spread on the table at one of the monthly renewals of the Armistice until the signing of the Treaty of Versailles. The small flag was carried by Reverend Dickson throughout his war service and used at all church parades held by him.

Finsthwaite

In October 1914, an ROH was placed in the porch at St Peter's Church, Finsthwaite by the vicar containing the names of five officers and sixteen men who were serving with the colours of the parish. Its current location is unknown. In March 1915, the list of former scholars of Finsthwaite School serving with the colours contained the names of twenty-seven old boys. The primary (mixed) school for 100 children was built in the small village in 1875.

A memorial tablet was unveiled in St Peter's Church to the memory of Second Lieutenant Robert Rawlinson, Border Regiment, the only son of John Baldwin and Theodora Rawlinson of Graythwaite Old Hall. Rawlinson, educated at Blundell's, Devon, was killed in action on 25 September 1915 at the Battle of Loos, and Mentioned in Despatches for gallant and distinguished services in the field.

Also inside the church, there is a plaque relating to the restoration of the War Memorial Clock in 2005. The clock and tenor bell, dedicated on 10 October 1920, were placed in the tower of the church by the inhabitants of the parish of Finsthwaite to remember the war dead. A second bell was placed in the tower by Clement Edward Hoyland (1869–1951) of Stott Park, Finsthwaite and his wife Louisa Eddie in memory of their son John Fraser Hoyland (1895–1916), Lancashire Fusiliers. He was killed in action at the Battle of Mouquet Farm, Thiepval, France on 26 September 1916, part of the Battle of the Somme.

There is an original battlefield cross with aluminium tags and with a Graves Registration Unit (GRU) tag at St Peter's Church with one man named: Lance Corporal Ernest Lewis (1896–1917), 1st/4th Seaforth Highlanders, of Stott Park, who died on 8 April 1917. The inscription is 'GRU / L/CPL E LEWIS / 1 SEAFORTHS / ORIGINAL CROSS'. On the outbreak of war Lewis, whose parents were Robert Lewis and Jane Urquhart Cook, had been working as under-butler to Lieutenant Colonel Timothy Fetherstonhaugh (1869–1945) of the College, Kirkoswald (about 9 miles from Penrith).

There is another original battlefield cross with aluminium tags at the church – in memory of Private Ernest Knowles (1889–1918), the Queen's Royal Surrey Regiment, who died on 13 April 1918. The inscription is 'GRU / PTE E KNOWLES / QRW SURREYS/ORIGINAL CROSS'. He was the son of Thomas and Annie Knowles (née Churchman) of Marsh Street, Barrow and lived at Finsthwaite (1901 census). He is buried in Meteren Military Cemetery, France. The cemetery contains 768 Commonwealth burials and commemorations of the First World War.

Private Franklin Benn Dearsley, 4th (Extra Reserve) Battalion, Lancashire Fusiliers, is buried at St Peter's. He died at home at Stott Park on 10 August 1916, aged 27, from Bright's disease, a condition involving chronic inflammation of the kidneys. The 4th (Extra Reserve) Battalion, Lancashire Fusiliers, remained in the UK for the duration of the war. At the time of Dearsley's enlistment, they formed part of the Barrow Garrison. There is no Medal Index Card for Franklin Dearsley. He did not serve overseas and therefore was not entitled to receive any medals. He also died before the Silver War Badge was instituted and these were not issued posthumously, but his next of kin would have received the commemorative Bronze Plaque and Scroll. Tragically, a week before Dearsley died he had got married. His occupation (1911 census) was footman domestic.

There was an ROH (twenty-one names) in the porch at St Peter's Church: 'Paper, in a glazed oak frame, a Union Jack with a scroll for the names and an inscription asking for the prayers of the congregation for those who are gone forth to fight for their King and Country, with vacant spaces for those yet to enlist.' It was unveiled on 29 October 1914 and is now lost.

Inside the church on the north wall of the chancel is a communion set of a brass chalice, two brass patens and a wooden cross, all in a glass case, with a framed explanation below. The chalice is made from the cap of an 18-pounder shell. The large paten is made from a 4.5in howitzer shell and the small paten from a 3in Austrian Berndorf shell. The cross is made from a plank of a pontoon bridge laid across the River Piave in Italy for the final allied assault in 1918.

Haverthwaite

The Haverthwaite Cross memorial lists fifteen men who fell in the Great War and the Haverthwaite Church memorial five. The five include

Second Lieutenant Fred Wilson, 9th Suffolk Regiment, of Low Wood, Haverthwaite, who is buried at the London Cemetery opposite High Wood on the Somme. He is likely to have fallen assaulting a German fortified trench system called the Quadrilateral near Ginchy on 15 September 1916.

There is a plaque at Haverthwaite Church in memory of Captain Richard Brooksbank Taylor (1885–1915), 1st Border. The son of Samuel and Gertrude Taylor of Birk Dault in Haverthwaite parish, he was killed at Gallipoli on 28 April 1915. At a patriotic concert in Haverthwaite School, 17 December 1915, the chairman paid a touching tribute to him. He also paid tribute to Private William Clark, missing since 27 August 1914, and Private Harry Edmondson, missing since 26 September 1914. He said he sincerely hoped that the two missing men would turn up.

By December 1915, Clark and Edmondson had been missing for over a year, so if truly missing should have been declared 'presumed dead' by then (normally that happened between six and twelve months after the missing date). That may mean they were really PoWs. As they are not on the Haverthwaite memorial, there is every hope that they survived and eventually returned home.

Hawkshead

At Hawkshead, there is a First World War memorial inside the church and a First World War ROH leather-bound book inside the church (the case is locked). It is a book of more than 120 pages containing the names of 119 men, 21 of whom fell. It was created in 1968, clearly a labour of love, beginning with an A-Z index followed by a page for each man with full personal and military biographical details under eleven headings and even the odd photograph. The book finishes with a summary of the fallen. One of the men included is Oscar Theodor Gnosspelius, who in 1925 married Barbara Collingwood, daughter of W.G. Collingwood.

The village cross in the churchyard near the lychgate was unveiled on 18 November 1920; there are twenty-one names from the First World War. This Scandinavian wheelhead cross was designed by W.G. Colling-wood and sculpted by his daughter Barbara. (There is reference to it being Anglo-Saxon but apparently it is not.)

In November 1916, 17-year-old Private James Hems (1899–1916), 1st/4th KO, was killed in action (Western Front). 'He would go,' said his mother Frances Hems of Edenbro, Ambleside (1899). Second Lieutenant Thomas Henry Irving, King's Liverpool Regiment, died on 19 August 1916. He was the son of the Reverend Canon Thomas Henry Irving and Margaret Anne Irving of Hawkshead Vicarage. In the *Hawkshead* magazine in 1916, the following was said: 'T.H. Irving was killed in

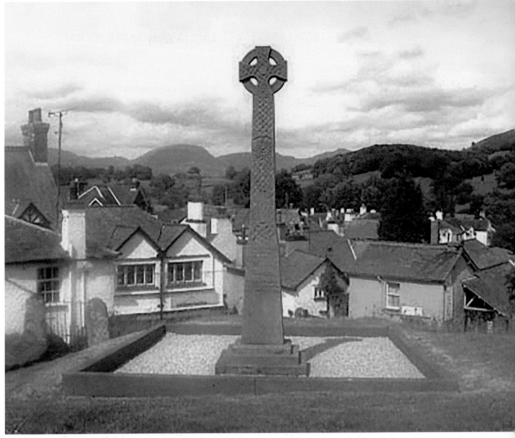

Hawkshead village cross, unveiled in 1920. (*cumbriawarmemorials*)

action while searching for his brother 2nd Lieutenant W.R. Irving who
was wounded the previous day while leading an attack on the German
lines.'

Private Frederick William Longmire, 25th Infantry Battalion,
Australian army, was killed in service in France on 10 June 1918. He
was the son of Nathan and Mary Longmire of Brown Cow Cottage,
Hawkshead. Private John Bowness Postlethwaite, Canadian Infantry,
died on 21 August 1917. He was the son of the late Isaac and Ann
Postlethwaite of The Square, Hawkshead.

Many places acquired field guns as memorials. At Hawkshead, the
gun came with a trench mortar, wire-cutters and other assorted hard-
ware. Another part of Hawkshead's memorial scheme was a recreation
ground opened on 30 July 1921. Coniston's trophy gun was placed outside the Ruskin Museum, Coniston. One night, veterans dragged it down
to Lake Coniston and chucked it in with the observation that they had
seen enough of such things in France. It was raised by local divers in
the 1960s.

Helsington parish

The artist Marion de Saumarez (1885–1978), who studied at the Académie Julian in Paris, created a mural in 1919 that was funded by Mrs Benson of Levens Hall near Kendal (at the time owned by Lieutenant Sir Alan Desmond Bagot who served in the Royal Horse Guards during the Great War and died in 1920). It was dedicated on 31 August 1919 at a service at St John's Church on the fellside above Brigsteer village in the parish of Helsington, attended by Reverend Frederick Salmon Vaughan. It is located on the east wall above the altar.

At the top of the wood panelling below the mural is the following inscription: 'TO THE GLORY OF GOD AND IN MEMORY OF ALL FAITHFUL DEPARTED ESPECIALLY THOSE WHO GAVE THEIR LIVES IN THE GREAT WAR 1914–1919.'

The artist used local girls as models for the twelve female angels in the painting. The angels with a wistful expression and flowers at their feet kneel facing the figure of Christ upon the cross. They appear to join in prayer with those gathered around the altar as they remember the faithful departed. The background of river, pastures and mountains clearly refers to the scene outside the church but there is no sign of life in the silent landscape, reflecting post-war desolation and communities

The mural by Marion de Saumarez was dedicated in 1919. (*warmemorials.myfastforum*)

deprived of their young men. The oil paint was applied in washes of colour, with virtually no impasto or visible brush marks, and matt in appearance, without varnish.

Langdale

On 26 September 1920, the slate war memorial in the churchyard of Holy Trinity Church in the valley of Langdale was unveiled (twenty-six names). The Langdale valley includes two villages, Chapel Stile and Elterwater, and a hamlet at High Close.

A wooden ROH with names in calligraphy can be found on the south wall of the nave at Holy Trinity Church. The names on the memorial total 144: 118 who served and returned and 26 who died. Reverend William Hayes of Langdale, in column four of the Langdale ROH, in 1917 was looking after a church army hut in France frequented by Windermere men.

South Lakeland's memorials continue to turn up in the most unlikely places. An example is the slab of stone in a small area of wood just east of Busk House, Little Langdale. There is a gate into the wood off the road (walking left from the Three Shires Inn, it is on the right-hand side

Slater Bridge, one of Lakeland's ancient pedestrian bridges, is on the route between Little Langdale and Tilberthwaite. It withstood floods in 2011. (*visitcumbria.com*)

of the road) by a small beck. This could be Busk Gill. It is about half a mile west of the Three Shires Inn along the road by Little Langdale Tarn. The nearest public transport would be Elterwater in Great Langdale.

The small community of Little Langdale consists of no more than a scattering of houses, a Post Office and a village pub. Nearby stands the picturesque footbridge known as Slater Bridge, an arch constructed of slate from the local quarries, built to connect Little Langdale with the slate quarries in the Tilberthwaite area.

Inscribed upon this memorial are the words: 'In Loving Memory / Denton / Lee / Died of Wounds / 1914–1918'. Second Lieutenant James Denton Lee (1890–1918), 10th Battalion Manchester Regiment, died of wounds in France on 22 January 1918 and is buried in the family plot in Lister Lane Cemetery, Halifax, West Yorkshire. The only son of William and Mary Lee, he was born into the family of a greengrocer in Halifax and when he was 8 years old his father died aged 36. In 1901, James Denton Lee was a resident scholar, aged 11, at the Crossley & Porter Orphanage on Manor Heath, Halifax (where ages ranged in 1901 from 8 to 16). Why the memorial in Langdale? A family member, Eddie Birchall, told the author in December 2015 that James's sister Katie Annie Lee, who never married, became a successful hairdresser in Blackpool. She paid for National Trust woodland to be planted and James's memorial to be placed there. She also paid for a seat to be placed in his memory at Trinity Academy, Halifax. Eddie Birchall said he could only assume that with Blackpool being close by, the family may have spent time in the Lake District. Crossley Orphanage was founded in 1864 and

Memorial to James Denton Lee. (*cumbrianwarmemorials*)

Wooden grave cross with black-painted dedications: 'R.I.P. / IN/MEMORY / OF /
No. 422532 CPL. J. STRONG / 29TH CDN. BN. / KILLED / IN / ACTION / 26/4/18'.
(*IWM*)

became Crossley & Porter School in 1919. Heath Grammar School and Crossley & Porter School (whose alumni include rugby union footballer Brian Moore) merged in 1984, becoming Crossley-Heath School. Today, Crossley-Heath is a grammar school serving the Halifax area. Ian Stuart Nicholson recently visited the site of the memorial as part of his work for the IWM. The stone of remembrance is well inside the clearing on the right-hand (or Three Shires Inn) side in Busk Wood. Busk Wood is on a minor road from the Three Shires Inn to the Wrynose Pass opposite Little Langdale Tarn.

There is a wooden cross on display at the Imperial War Museum, London from the grave of Corporal Joshua Strong (1889–1918), 29th Canadian Infantry, who was killed in action on 26 April 1918. His parents, Joseph and Mary Strong, were from Elterwater, and in 1911 he lived in Elterwater and worked as a quarryman. His remains are buried at Bellacourt Military Cemetery, Riviere, France. This original grave-marker, 702mm high and 413mm wide, was replaced after the war by an inscribed headstone provided by the Imperial (now Commonwealth) War Graves Commission. The IWM Joshua Strong collection also includes a Next of Kin Memorial plaque, a headed letter from Buckingham Palace, an OHMS envelope with typescript '422532 Pte J. Strong' [later promoted to corporal] and a plain square envelope containing the plaque itself, a wallet, wristwatch and Canadian Memorial Cross.

Longsleddale parish

Fifteen men are named on a board inside St Mary's Church in the parish of Longsleddale: twelve served and returned; three died. Longsleddale includes the hamlet of Sadgill, about 7 miles east of Windermere.

Lance Corporal George Cragg (1895–1916), 11th Border, a farm labourer who lived at Toms Howe, Longsleddale (1911 census), was killed in action on 26 June 1916 (Western Front). He is buried at Authuile Military Cemetery in France. Private Robert Gilpin (1896–1915), 8th Border, was killed by a shot to the head on 22 November 1915 (Western Front). He is buried at Lancashire Cottage Cemetery, Comines-Warneton, Hainaut in Belgium. Private Roger Wilson (1896–1917), Canadian Expeditionary Force, died on 9 April 1917 at the Battle of Vimy Ridge. He was the eldest son of William and Alice Wilson of Netherhouse, Longsleddale. The *WG* of 21 April 1917 reported:

His platoon commander writes: 'During our attack on the 9th at about 9.20am, Roger was advancing with his gun crew under very heavy shell fire. A shell made a direct hit on the gun and crew, killing Roger outright, wounding two others and smashing the gun.

Looking up from Sadgill. (*mountain-bike-cumbria*)

Lancashire Cottage Cemetery, 1919. (*ww1cemeteries*)

Your boy suffered no pain whatever. He was a splendid type of young soldier, always cheerful and attentive to his duties and a favourite with all his comrades.'

Low Wray

A war memorial was unveiled at St Margaret's Church, Low Wray, reported the *WG* on 2 April 1921. Five men are named, including Private Edward James Dugdale (1898–1917), Royal Medical Corps, of Low Wray Farm. He died on 8 March 1917 in Blackpool of pneumonia and bronchitis following influenza. Private Richard George Dugdale (1896–1917), 1st Lincs Yeomanry, of Ambleside, who enlisted in Penrith, died at sea on 15 April 1917. *Arcadian*, a passenger liner constructed in 1899 at Vickers in Barrow for the London to Australia route, served with the Royal Navy in the First World War and was sunk by *UC-74* while 26 miles north-east of the Greek island of Milos. Dugdale, buried at Mikra Memorial, Greece, was among the 297 people who died. Many of the dead were cooks and stokers who were working below decks.

The church has a brass plaque memorial to Lieutenant Brian Crossley, 2nd Battalion Highland Light Infantry, of Ambleside. He was killed at Festubert in May 1915. Low Wray Church is now closed for public worship and is in the care of the National Trust. The memorials are safe inside.

Lowick Bridge

There is a pillar surmounted on a four-stepped base in the churchyard at St Luke's Church, Lowick Bridge. Twelve men died, including Private James Edward Leck (1891–1916), 1/4th KO, a stone builder's apprentice of Lowick Bridge, and Private Robert Shuttleworth (1877–1917), 2nd Border, of Lowick Green, a labourer who enlisted in April 1916 aged 39. Shuttleworth died from wounds on 8 October 1917. British Army Service Records list his effects (29 October 1917) as including two discs, one pipe, four keys, one knife, one cap badge, a pencil, one pouch, one razor, one piece of shrapnel and one bag. His brothers (half-blood) included John Shuttleworth of Hollin Hall near Ulverston, and his sister (half-blood) Hannah Barrow lived at Burblethwaite Hall, Cartmel Fell. Meanwhile, the *Whitehaven News* reported on 18 July 1918 that a mother in Lowick had committed suicide at the prospect of her son's call-up.

Penny Bridge

There is a brass plaque with marble surround and foliate border with roses at each corner at St Mary the Virgin Church, Oak Vale, Penny Bridge. The names (twenty-one) are in two columns. Private William

The parish of Lowick is made up of several small hamlets including Woodgate, Lowick Bridge and Lowick Green. (*warmemorials.myfastforum*)

Leviston (1891–1916), 4th KO, of Penny Bridge, whose father was George Leviston, was reported wounded and missing on 31 July 1915 and reported killed in action on 6 May 1916. He was formerly a coachbuilder. Also at the church is a wooden lychgate in honour of the men who served in the Great War.

Tottlebank Baptist Church is in a minor dead end lane off the Spark Bridge to Penny Bridge back road. Six names are listed on the brass plaque erected to the memory of the young male members of the church and congregation who gave their lives. On the east wall of the church is a wooden board in honour of those forty-seven men who served in the Great War. Private Thomas Ramsden (1884–1914), also remembered at Colton Church north of Tottlebank, was killed in action on 21 October 1914. He was born in Lancaster, son of George, a matting weaver, and Angela Ramsden, and number ten of their thirteen children. They moved to a property that had been Penny Bridge Furnace on the Colton Parish side of the River Crake before moving to Highworth, Wiltshire. Thomas Ramsden and his twin brother Herbert (1884–1986) left home (then Highworth) at the age of 16 to fight in the Boer War, so at the outbreak of the First World War they were immediate volunteers, Thomas serving with the 2nd Lancashire Fusiliers and Herbert with the Wiltshire Regiment. In the 1920s, Herbert – who is on the Tottlebank served and returned memorial – emigrated to Australia. He suffered, as a result of his service, from severe hearing impairment and died on 8 January 1986, aged 101. Gunner Frederick Ramsden, Royal Garrison Artillery, on the Tottlebank served and returned memorial, was a younger brother of the twins.

Oakbank

There is a wooden bench in the hamlet of Oakbank, between Burneside and Skelsmergh, installed in 2014. It has a brass plaque inscribed: '1914–18 CENTENARY / IN MEMORY OF THE OAKBANK MEN WHO GAVE / THEIR LIVES IN THE / FIRST WORLD WAR'.

Rusland

There is a wooden framed ROH at St Paul's Church, Rusland with a wreath above under the dedication and shields down either side. The lettering is in black with red capitals and the fallen marked with a cross. Thirty-four men of Rusland are remembered: thirty served and returned; four died.

Staveley

There is a plaque at the recreation ground gates commemorating the men and women of Staveley who helped their country to victory (there are no names on the memorial). The land was purchased by subscription in 1922 to provide a recreation ground for the people of Staveley.

The Staveley cross at the Kentmere Road/Brow Lane junction names thirty-two men. Some of the soldiers were brought up at The Abbey children's home in Staveley (closed in 1956); about thirty-two children were being cared for there in 1905. In October 1915, twenty children from South Shields were brought to The Abbey home where they were to stay for the duration of the war. The buildings in which they lived were taken over by the government.

Andrew Hill (1886–1914), a native of Garforth in Yorkshire, had lived at Main Street, Staveley, for eight years. He was postman for the Kentmere Valley. A reservist, he immediately joined the 1st West Yorks and was killed on 20 September 1914. His battalion attacked the Germans at Troyon on the River Aisne. Their casualties that day amounted to 630 officers and men. He is buried in the French Communal Cemetery at Villers-en-Prayères, along with thirty-two other British soldiers, and is remembered on the Staveley cross. His name is also engraved on the war memorial plaque at Stricklandgate Post Office, Kendal.

There is a brass plaque memorial inside St Mary's Church, Staveley to Corporal Edwin Featherstone Martindale (1873–1918), 10th Battalion Canadians, who fell in action in France on 22 January 1918. The son of Joseph Anthony and Mary Ann Martindale of Staveley, he is buried at Fosse Communal Cemetery Extension, Pas de Calais, France.

Troutbeck

The Troutbeck Cross at Jesus Church, Troutbeck was erected by the inhabitants of Troutbeck in memory of twelve men who gave their lives in the Great War. It is a Celtic cross on a three-stepped base. Behind the organ inside Jesus Church is a First World War bronze plaque set on wood inscribed with twelve names.

The Troutbeck First World War Bells Brass is inscribed as follows:

THE PEAL OF CHIMING BELLS IN THIS TOWER / WAS PRESENTED BY ARTHUR BROOK DUNLOP / OF THE HOWE AND HIS DAUGHTER INGHA, IN / LOVING MEMORY OF HIS ONLY TWO SONS / ERIC AND LINDSAY WHO GAVE THEIR LIVES / IN THE GREAT WAR, AS OFFICERS IN / HIS MAJESTY'S FORCES, THE FORMER IN 1917, THE LATTER IN 1916.

The two casualties are also commemorated on the bronze plaque and the churchyard cross.

The Ecclerigg First World War ROH in Jesus Church is in a glazed wooden frame. Seventy-three names are on the memorial: sixty-seven served and returned and six died. Its previous location was St Andrew's Church, Ecclerigg, Troutbeck Bridge. The Troutbeck ROH is in the porch of Jesus Church, in a glazed wooden frame. Ninety-four names are on the memorial: seventy-nine served and returned; fifteen died. The ROH gives three extra casualties to the plaque in the church: J. Henry Mallinson, J. Hayhurst and Harry Smith.

Witherslack

Second Lieutenant John William Stanley (1886–1917), Lancashire Fusiliers, killed in action at Messines Ridge, Flanders on 7 June 1917, is named on a family military service memorial plaque at St Paul's Church, Witherslack. The upper brass names Charles James Fox Stanley (1808–1884), his wife Fanny Augusta Stanley (1810–1884), their second son Douglas James George Stanley (1847–1877) and their third son Robert Hamilton Stanley (1849–1900). The lower brass names their eldest son Charles Edward Henry Stanley (1843–1909) and John William Stanley.

CHAPTER TWENTY-ONE

Prisoners of War

Mr and Mrs George Dixon of White Moss Cottages, Grasmere had five sons fighting at the front. Their second son Henry Dixon (d.1918), Royal Welsh Fusiliers, enlisted in November 1915. In just the next two-and-a-half years, he would go on to serve in India, Mesopotamia, South Africa and finally France. He was captured by the Germans and imprisoned in Limburg in the region of Hessen, Germany. He later died from pneumonia in hospital in Tournai, Belgium. (Some PoWs were at several camps while still registered as being at Limburg.)

Draw Well Farm, Crosthwaite (built around 1640), was home to the Inman family for more than 300 years. William Walker Inman (1894–1917), the eldest child of James and Rebecca Inman, died in 1917 as a PoW. His family believe he was a PoW first in Wahn camp, south-east of Cologne, and then in Limburg camp. His name appears on the wooden memorial cross that now stands adjacent to the organ in St Mary's Church, Crosthwaite. His brothers James Edward and Cuthbert Pearson were the last to live at the farm in 1969.

Private Fred Kendall (d.1918), 8th Border, whose name is on the Hawkshead War Memorial and the slate tablet at St Oswald's, was the son of Mr and Mrs Edward Kendall of Score Cragg, Grasmere. His wife lived in Keswick and he enlisted in Keswick in September 1915 where he was a gardener. Private Kendall had previously served with his regiment at the Battle of the Somme. He was taken prisoner on 11 April 1918 during the Battle of the Lys. For the next five months, he was held at Limburg where he died from starvation on 4 September 1918. He was buried at Terlincthun British Cemetery on the outskirts of Boulogne, France.

Limburg was mainly used for Irish PoWs, part of a plan by Germany and Sir Roger Casement (1864–1916), a former British diplomat who was stripped of his knighthood in 1916 shortly before his execution for treason, to involve Irish nationalists in an 'Irish Brigade' against Britain. In November 2007, the German town of Dietkirchen restored and re-dedicated a Celtic cross erected in May 1917 to the memory of forty-five First World War Irish soldiers who died at Limburg.

Limburg PoW camp (capacity 12,000). The Germans were sceptical of Casement but aware of the military advantage they could gain from an uprising in Ireland.

The showers in Limburg camp.

Private Frederick Mallinson (1894–1978), Border, of Russmickle Farm, Crosthwaite, who had a rifle wound in his body, was taken prisoner at Grandcourt, Somme on 18 November 1916; by himself, according to his records kept at TNA. He was taken to a church, just behind the lines, where he found about thirty other British prisoners, and he stayed in the church for two days. A German Red Cross man put a field dressing on his wound. Mallinson said:

> My jack-knife was taken away, but not my pay-back or money. I, personally, got no food, because I was unable to get up and get it. Some soup was brought in, and the other men had it. We had to lie on the floor with no covering at all.

Mallinson left this church and spent one night at Cambrai Hospital, France. He received proper medical attention and food and was well treated.

On 22 November, he left Cambrai for Germany. There was a party of about twenty-one British; the rest on the train, which was a Red Cross train, were Germans. He was put in hospital in the city of Wesel on 24 November, where he remained for three weeks. Only the very worst cases out of the twenty-one were attended to; the others were neglected, such as Mallinson.

After he had been there two days, he was given a postcard to write home. On 14 December, he was taken to Münster I Westphalia PoW camp with two others, where he remained until 18 February 1917. While there, he recovered from his wound. He said:

> I used to go out about three days a week to work, but received no pay. It was general fatigue work, and not very hard. We were very badly fed, and I received my first parcel here. I received about eight altogether while I was there, and I lived on them. These were food parcels, but contained no clothes. I got an overcoat from the Germans, but no other clothes.

Mallinson received his first letter from home while at Münster. He said: 'On the 18th February 1917, I was sent out on kommando by myself to Kommando 78, a sawmill on the outskirts of Gladbeck. There were about fourteen British and twenty-two French there when I got there.' He remained there until 2 April 1917. The food was bad, but parcels came regularly. The work was very heavy at the sawmill, carrying logs of trees about. The hours were 6.30am to 6.15pm, six days a week, for a payment of 90 pfennig (less than one German mark) per day.

Around 2 April 1917, he was removed with ten British and two Frenchmen to Kommando 66 situated at Hafen close to Barop, north-west Germany, where the discipline was not very severe, although the food was worse. He remained there until he escaped on 6 October 1918 with one other man, Private Smith of the Canadian Mounted Rifles. It took them six weeks to reach Holland.

Frederick Mallinson, whose parents were Robert Mallinson and Mary Jane Hogg, died in 1978 in Lancaster. His brother, Lance Corporal Robert Henry Mallinson (1896–1917), 11th Border, died on 25 September 1917 (Western Front) and is named in St Mary's Church, Crosthwaite.

Private Thomas Joseph Priest, 1st Battalion KO, of Field Foot, Grasmere, and Corporal George Allan Wilson of Above Beck Cottage, Grasmere were PoWs. Wilson was awarded the Long Service and Good Conduct Medal in 1919. It is a service medal awarded to personnel in various branches of the military of the UK and the territories that are or were at some point a part of the British Empire or Commonwealth of Nations. Private Alex Smith, part of the King's Liverpool Regiment, of Blue Hill, Ambleside succumbed to starvation, the *Barrow News* reported on 30 November 1918. He had been a PoW in Germany and was released. However, he collapsed when he reached his base.

In total, there were forty-nine PoWs from the Royal Lancaster Regiment, 1914–18.

German PoWs in South Lakeland

When war was declared, there was no system in place on either side for dealing with PoWs. Camps were hastily set up according to need. Many camps were built from scratch but existing buildings were also utilized. The author's listing of camps was drawn from official lists found at TNA, all from 1918 or 1919. So any camps no longer in use when the lists were drawn up are not in those lists.

In September 1918, ten German prisoners arrived at Sandside railway station under the charge of a platoon of Royal Defence Corps and were marched to their quarters at the workhouse. An interpreter accompanied them to arrange matters and the whole body started work in the harvest fields at Greenhead. Sandside station served the hamlet and quarries of Sandside. A Furness Railway local passenger train service (known locally as the 'Kendal Tommy' after one of the longest-serving members of the regular crew) ran from Arnside to Kendal, via Sandside and Hincaster, between 1876 and its withdrawal in May 1942 when the station also closed to passengers. During the Second World War, a new utility bus was put into service. The land referred to as the workhouse would have been in Milnthorpe. The parent camp was a disused mill in Leigh, Lancashire.

Leigh was also the parent camp of the PoW camp at Stainton Sidings, between Dalton-in-Furness and Lindal-in-Furness. The Stainton mineral branch of the Furness Railway, which opened in 1866, started at Stainton Branch Junction between Dalton and Lindal and ended at Stainton with Adgarley, a quarry village near Urswick in South Lakeland. The Stainton Sidings camp was closed in May 1919 and the prisoners taken to Leigh.

Other PoW camps in South Lakeland included Biggar Bank, Barrow (opened in April 1919); North End, Barrow; and Kendal (opened early in 1918). Biggar Bank, North End and Kendal were inspected on 17 and 18 June 1919. All reports – by the Swiss Legation of Carlton House Terrace, London – were very good. At North End, German privates were appointed as interpreter and camp clerks. At Kendal, the prisoners were *Unteroffizier* (the equivalent in anglophone armed forces of sergeant or staff sergeant) who had volunteered to work. There were nineteen prisoners at Kendal on 23 June 1919, where the camp occupied part of the premises of the workhouse, and fifty at North End. Biggar Bank and North End were formerly occupied by British troops and were typical specimens of 'hutted' camps.

CHAPTER TWENTY-TWO

The End of the Struggle

For those on the home front, the 1918 August Bank Holiday had lightened the general burden of war-weariness. Pre-war numbers of cars flocked into the Lake District. Even so, there was no let-up in the war news. The Great War ended with the Armistice on 11 November 1918.

At Windermere, the first flag was raised on the lofty pole at Rigg's Windermere Hotel (now the Windermere Hotel), which during the Second World War was the home of Ashville College of Harrogate, North Yorkshire. Later in the day, Canon Euston John Nurse – at one of the many victory services throughout the district – gave thanks for the victory over Germany. In Grasmere, the news of the Armistice was received with feelings of great relief and restrained gladness. Flags were put out all through the village and there was much congratulation and hand-shaking in the street. When the ringers could be collected, the church bells were rung in the evening. Impromptu dancing occurred at Coniston and a general holiday was given to workers at Cropper's Paper Mill and at K Shoes. Schoolchildren at Troutbeck had the day off.

At Lakeside Jubilee Institute, Finsthwaite, all the villagers from Finsthwaite were invited to a party given by the man who lived at Stock Park Mansion on the south-west shore of Lake Windermere. The children were given their tea first, and then watched a Punch and Judy show. Later, the adults arrived and there was dancing. Everyone joined in, young and old alike.

After the signing of the formal peace treaty – the Treaty of Versailles – on 28 June 1919, the government decreed that 19 July 1919 was to be the National Day of Celebration. In Broadgate meadow, Grasmere, there is a large oak tree. Beside it is a small slate boulder explaining that the oak was planted by Canon Rawnsley on Peace Day, 19 July 1919, when all the villagers of Grasmere and district gathered in Broadgate meadow to celebrate the signing of the peace treaty.

Disabled, a poem by Wilfred Owen (1893–1918), explores the effects of war on those who live through it by comparing the present life of an injured soldier to his past hopes and accomplishments. The women he joined up to impress are ignoring him and he feels that his courage means nothing to them now he is in a wheelchair. Attitudes had to change. In his book *An Imperial Obligation: Industrial Villages for Partially Disabled Soldiers* (London: Grant Richards, 1917), Thomas Mawson advanced a scheme for purpose-built villages to house disabled ex-servicemen. Although he received widespread support, his ideas were opposed by the Ministry of Pensions and only Westfield Village, Lancaster was built, the funds raised through private donations.

The first superintendent of Westfield Village was Captain John Fraser Dawson. Originally from the Scottish Highlands, he had been a police sergeant at Wigton, 17 miles from Workington, and later a grocer and provisions dealer (his original trade in Scotland) at Workington before the war. While at Workington, he joined the TF in the Rifle Volunteers in which he was successively sergeant, armourer sergeant and quarter-master sergeant. He was also a deacon of Workington Congregational Church. When the Lonsdale Battalion was formed, he was appointed quartermaster and was later posted to the RAF. He died at Lancaster on 15 April 1926 and is buried at Wigton Cemetery. PoW Private Fred Watson (b.1879) of Cobden Street, Padiham, Lancashire is believed to be the first occupant of the 1st Battalion Cottage Le Cateau on Westfield.

Bibliography

Primary sources

Bates, Martha, *Snagging Turnips and Scaling Muck* (Helm Press, 2001).

Bostridge, Mark, *The Fateful Year: England 1914* (2014).

Burk, Kathleen, *Troublemaker: The Life and History of A.J.P. Taylor* (2002).

Chorlton, Martyn, *Cumbria Airfields in the Second World War, including the Isle of Man* (Countryside Books, 2006).

Clark, David, *The Labour Movement in Westmorland* (2014).

Cox & Co., *List of British Officers Taken Prisoner, 1914–18* (London Stamp Exchange, 1988).

Crewdson, Richard (ed.), *Dorothea's War: The Diaries of a First World War Nurse* (Weidenfeld & Nicolson, 2013).

Crossley, Barbara, *The Other Ambleside* (Titus, 2000).

Cumbria Federation of Women's Institutes, *Cumbria, Within Living Memory* (Countryside Books, 1994).

Foley, Michael, *Britain's Railway Disasters: Fatal Accidents from the 1830s to the Present Day* (2014).

Greenhaugh, W., *Broughton-in-Furness & the Duddon Valley* (1989).

Harris, W.L. and Talbot, Edward, *Recollections of Oxenholme* (London & North Western Railway Society, 1994).

Kendal, H.G.G., *The War Work of Auxiliary Hospitals and Voluntary Aid Detachments of Cumberland, Westmorland and parts of North-West Lancashire* (T. Wilson & Son, 1921).

Kutzer, M. Daphne, *Beatrix Potter, Writing in Code* (Routledge, 2003).

The Lonsdale Battalion, Border Regiment, September 1914 to June 1915 (Chas. Thurnam and Sons, 11 English Street, Carlisle, 1915).

Marshall, J.D. and Davies-Shiel, M., *The Lake District at Work, Past and Present* (David & Charles, 1971).

Marshall, J.D. and Walton, John K., *The Lake Counties from 1830 to the mid-20th Century* (Manchester University Press, 1981).

Mitchell, W.R., *Lakeland Dalesfolk* (Dalesman, 1983).

Morris, Joseph, *German Air-Raids on Britain, 1914–1918*.

Newman, Vivien, *We Also Served: The Forgotten Women of the First World War* (Pen & Sword, 2014).

Nurse, E.J., *History of Windermere Parish Church* (1908).

Pearce, Cyril, *Comrades in Conscience* (Francis Boutle, 2001).

Pevsner, Nikolaus, *The Buildings of North Lancashire* (Penguin, 1969).

Robinson, Peter, *Railwaymen Remembered* (Cumbrian Railways Association, 2008).

Rolt, L.T.C., *Red for Danger: The Classic History of British Railway Disasters* (1966).

Scott, S.H., *The Story of the Old Homesteads and 'Statesman' Families of Troutbeck by Windermere* (Archibald Constable & Co.).

Simpson, Jacqueline and Roud, Stephen, *A Dictionary of English Folklore* (2000).
Storey, Neil R. and Housego, Molly, *Women in the First World War* (Shire Publications).
Wadham, W.F.A. and Crossley, J., *The Fourth Battalion The King's Own (Royal Lancaster Regiment) and the Great War* (1920, second edition 1935).
Waymark, Janet, *Thomas Mawson: Life, Gardens and Landscapes* (2009).
Webb, Sarah, *The First World War with IWMs* (Hodder, 2014).
Western, Robert, *The Kendal and Windermere Railway, Gateway to the Lakes* (Oakwood Press, 2012).
Wharton, Edith, *The Book of the Homeless* (Scribner, New York, 1916).
Wilson, Paul N., *The Gunpowder Mills of Westmorland and Furness* (read at the Science Museum, London on 5 February 1964).
Woodward, Rachel and Winter, Trish, *Sexing the Soldier: The Politics of Gender and the Contemporary British Army*.
Wrigley, C.J., *A.J.P. Taylor: Radical Historian of Europe* (2006).

Newspapers and other publications
Barrow News
Bolton News
Carlisle Journal
Cumberland News
Cumbria magazine, May 1955
Daily Mail
Daily Mirror
Daily News
Daily Telegraph
Fell and Rock Climbing Club Journals, 1914, 1915, 1916, 1917, 1918, 1919
Flight magazine
Hawkshead magazine
Lakes Herald
London Gazette
Manchester Guardian
Millom Gazette
Penrith Observer
The Scotsman
The Times
West Cumberland Times
Westmorland Gazette
Whitehaven News
Wigton Advertiser
Yorkshire Evening Post
Yorkshire Post and Leeds Intelligencer

Online sources
airfieldinformationexhange.org (lists Great War places of internment/PoW camps)
ancestry.co.uk
British Newspaper Archive
cultrans.com (Cumberland & Westmorland Newspaper Archives)
cumbria-industries.org.uk
cumbrianwarmemorials.blogspot.co.uk
www.iwm.org.uk (Imperial War Museum)

ppu.org.uk (Peace Pledge Union)
ramc-ww1.com (RAMC in the Great War)
www.warmemorials.org (War Memorials Online)
whitefeatherdiaries.org
yorkshirereporter.co.uk
Museums, etc.
British Library, London
Cumbria's Museum of Military Life, Carlisle
IWM, London
The National Archives, Kew (TNA)
V&A display, London: 'Beatrix Potter: The Land, the Seasons and the War'

Index